A SONG OF LONGING

Kay Kaufman Shelemay

University of Illinois Press

Urbana and Chicago

A SONG OF LONGING

AN ETHIOPIAN JOURNEY

© 1991 by the Board of Trustees of the University of Illinois
Manufactured in the United States of America
C 5 4 3 2 1

This book is printed on acid-free paper.

Library of Congress Cataloging-in-Publication Data

Shelemay, Kay Kaufman.
    A song of longing : an Ethiopian journey / by Kay Kaufman
Shelemay.
        p. cm.
    Includes bibliographical references and index.
    ISBN 0-252-01798-6 (cloth)
    1. Falashas—Social life and customs. 2. Shelemay, Kay Kaufman—
Journeys—Ethiopia. 3. Ethiopia—Description and
travel—1945–1980. 4. Ethiopia—History—Revolution, 1974—Personal
narratives. 5. Ethiopia—Ethnic relations. I. Title.
DS135.E75S54 1991
963.07—dc20   90-24294
                                                                      CIP

To Jack

The season of glad songs has come (Song of Songs 2:12)

CONTENTS

ACKNOWLEDGMENTS

I am grateful to the family, friends, and colleagues who encouraged me in this venture. I thank my parents, Lillian and Raymond Kaufman, for their enthusiastic support and for preserving materials that enabled me to write this book. A residency at the Bellagio Conference and Study Center of the Rockefeller Foundation in 1989 provided a period of peace and reflection during which much of the final text was written.

I thank Adrienne Fried Block, Hedy and Jerry Bookin-Weiner, David Burrows, John Harbeson, Ellen T. Harris, Marilyn Heldman, and Nancy Risser for insightful comments upon earlier drafts of this manuscript. University of Illinois Press Executive Editor Judith McCulloh provided invaluable critical feedback and enlisted anonymous readers for the review process who made their own excellent suggestions, many of which I have gratefully incorporated.

The Shelemay family and many others in Ethiopia shared the experiences recounted here; I hope that this book betrays neither their memories nor their trust. Jack Shelemay's memories are intertwined with mine throughout these pages, and it is to him that this book is lovingly dedicated.

INTRODUCTION

When I went to Ethiopia in the summer of 1973, I was an enthusiastic young woman of twenty-five planning to do research for my doctoral dissertation. I had spent most of my life involved with the performance and study of Western classical music until a chance encounter in 1970 with Ethiopian music left me consumed with the goal of living in Ethiopia and studying its musical traditions. Although I felt some trepidation about the trip, I thought myself reasonably well prepared by three years of graduate study for what I assumed would be the usual ups and downs of a field experience abroad.

I spent nearly two and a half years in Ethiopia, returning to the United States at the end of 1975 to complete my Ph.D. Since then I have worked as a professor of music, teaching in universities and publishing scholarly books and articles. Over the years I efficiently partitioned the outcome of my Ethiopian research into traditional, manageable chunks—a bit here for an article about a new system of musical notation conceived by an urban folklore orchestra, more there for book-length studies of Ethiopian liturgical music.

Until now, my publications have adhered to the generally accepted conventions of scholarly writing, most notably in maintaining clear boundaries between what I believed to be strictly personal experiences and those situations related to my studies. While I was always aware of my role as a cultural translator and tried to let my research associates be heard both through quotation and transcriptions of the music and texts they performed, I felt constrained to present my own activities and opinions only as they related directly to the gathering and interpretation of research materials.

Only occasionally did I mention, in a rather distanced manner, the impact of political events upon my research schedule and findings, most directly in the introduction to *Music, Ritual, and Falasha History* ([1986]1989). There I discussed briefly the interruption of my village research by the near-simultaneous start of the Ethiopian revolution and my marriage to a member of the permanent expatriate community in the Ethiopian capital. But in largely severing the research data (and my resulting interpretations) from the broader context in which I conducted that research, I believe I told only part of the story.

I began working on *A Song of Longing* in 1986, at first planning to write a more accessible account of my controversial findings about the Falasha religious tradition. But almost as soon as I began to write, other issues began to surface. To speak honestly about my Falasha research, I realized, I had to explore the relationship between my personal and professional experience in the field and the manner in which the two were inseparable.

From the start I struggled with the fact that I wanted to write a book that would not fit into an established literary or scholarly category. The problem had implications for both publication prospects and my career. Not only might I write a book that would be unpublishable, but I would discuss subjects almost certainly considered irrelevant or embarrassing in the world of serious musical scholarship. In the end, the fact that anthropologists had been tackling similar questions concerning both the nature of ethnography and the style and content of ethnographic writing (Marcus and Fischer 1986; Clifford and Marcus 1986) encouraged me in my own venture. Then, too, with the security of tenure I was able to approach this book as a challenge rather than a risk. Thus, as *A Song of Longing* goes to press some five years after its inception, it is intentionally experimental. It sits between genres, being at once an explication of the ethnomusicological work I did in Ethiopia from 1973 to 1975 and a reflection on the extraordinary personal experiences that shaped that research process. It may be read on its own or as a companion to my more conventional scholarly books and articles, listed in the Selected Bibliography, on many aspects of Ethiopian music.

I constructed this text from a combination of sources, including my field notes and journals, which were most detailed for the fall of 1973 and for 1975. I had suspended my personal journal in January 1974, when I left Ethiopia briefly for my wedding. After my return a few months later, further rural fieldwork had become impossible because of the advent of the revolution. Though I soon became aware that I was an observer of extraordinary changes in Ethiopia, the nature of these changes and my own vulnerability left me uneasy about recording the events that transpired. From then on, I documented only the formal fieldwork sessions that I carried out in Addis Ababa.

As both telephone and mail communications to the outside world became more undependable and vulnerable to censors, I was fortunate to have opportunities to send some frank and detailed letters to my parents through protected diplomatic channels. These letters became my primary venue for sharing my experiences with my family and one of the few contexts in which I could vent my growing frustration. My mother saved all of these letters, providing me with a source for reconstructing both the events of 1974–75 and my reaction to them at the time.

Though it is often said that memory is no substitute for a written record, in the course of writing this book I have been surprised at how many events and conversations remain sharply etched in my mind. I have also been fortunate in being able to draw upon the memories of others, most notably those of my husband, Jack Shelemay. Much of chapter 4 has been compiled from the many tales told to me by Jack and his family about their life in Aden. Parts of chapters 6, 7, and 10, which contain considerable detail about our individual and shared experiences during the Ethiopian revolution, were drafted during a residency at the Rockefeller Foundation Study and Conference Center at Bellagio in 1989. Guided only by a brief chronology published by the Ethiopian government (1975), Jack and I systematically talked our way through the revolution, recalling what had happened. We found this process painful yet cathartic; through it we relived what had seemed to be the dissolution of our lives. In general, we found that our memories of the larger events converged, though we disagreed sometimes in our interpretations of their meaning and impact. During these conversations I made detailed notes that I used when writing the relevant chapters. Over the last several years, I have also done some informal interviewing with other members of the Shelemay family, cross-checking their memories and their responses to various events. All of this is woven into the text.

This is a book about real people and real places. Often I have had to balance my perception of the truth and attention to detail against a need for privacy, both my own and others. Many of the situations I discuss are sensitive and in some cases I have had to disguise the participants. When appropriate I have provided pseudonyms for individuals outside the Shelemay family. I have tried not to sanitize or romanticize this reconstruction while seeking to convey the power of the experience, although no doubt the passage of time has highlighted some memories and dulled others. Of the family members mentioned in these pages, only Jack and my parents read the manuscript prior to publication. Although they offered corrections for a few factual errors, they in no way exercised editorial control. The decision to include or exclude material was strictly my own and I am solely responsible for the results.

The account in the following pages is by no means exhaustive, but it does explicitly acknowledge a complexity of experience otherwise obscured by conventional scholarly distance. The course of events framing a research process directly contributes to its outcome, most strikingly here, to the surprising conclusions stemming from my study of the sacred music of the Beta Israel or the Falasha, now known as the Ethiopian Jews. The advent of the Ethiopian revolution terminated my village fieldwork with the Beta Israel and pushed me toward other areas of inquiry, including studies of the Ethiopian Christian musical tradition.

The revolution altered the nature of my relationship to Ethiopia and its people, ending many friendships while reaffirming others. These events affected me profoundly and propelled me into new ways of seeing the world. They continued to transform my perspectives even after I left the country. For this reason, although most of this book recounts events that took place between 1973 and 1975, I have extended the chronology forward in chapter 9 to explore the ethical dilemmas and political conflicts that emerged from findings made after I left Ethiopia.

I was an accidental witness to a stunning series of changes in the Horn of Africa, and in the lives of communities and individuals with whom I was deeply involved. In part because of these events, my experience in the field in many ways inverted the conventional fieldwork pattern, usually presented as moving from initial dislocation, through increasing accommodation, to achievement of a modified insider status. In contrast, my first six months as a researcher in Ethiopia were remarkably smooth and productive. I was welcomed warmly by the Beta Israel community, who from the beginning facilitated all aspects of my research.

From its beginning, my relationship with Jack Shelemay also gave me a unique vantage point. As both researcher and permanent resident I lived a life that cut across communities and social classes. I had access both to traditional Ethiopian society and to its more cosmopolitan elements. Later I was to witness the impact of revolutionary change on both native Ethiopians and on the permanent foreign community that had long made Ethiopia its home. This book tells all these stories, not so much to chronicle a revolution which has been charted in considerable detail elsewhere (most recently in Harbeson 1988), but to convey the ethos of an experience in its thrall.

This book differs from conventional ethnography in several ways, most notably in its considerable detail concerning my marriage to Jack Shelemay and our life as part of the Adenite Jewish community in Addis Ababa. Recent ethnographic literature has shown great concern with the construction and presentation of the "Other," both in relationship to the ethnographer (Fabian

1983) and with regard to the informant's interior life (Crapanzano 1980). Though I married into a group separate from the ones that I studied, this personal experience was in every sense as rich a cross-cultural challenge as my fieldwork in more traditional contexts. The Shelemays, too, were in many ways the Other. I hope that the following pages make clear the ways in which my adjustment to life in their compound on Benin Sefer both paralleled and complicated my entry into the other Ethiopian worlds around me.

In the years since I left Ethiopia, I have become increasingly aware that I had a rare, insider's exposure to the distinctive social and cultural life that exists in the developing world at the intersection between foreigners present on a permanent or long-term basis and natives of the country itself. Various terms have been applied to describe both the widespread phenomenon and the constituent subgroups of these multiplex communities, including the "third culture" (Useem, Useem, and Donoghue 1963), "strangers" (Simmel [1908]1950), and "marginal men" (Park 1928).

My exposure to the third culture as its existed in Ethiopia was in part predictable. Most fieldworkers have contact with others from their home society when in the field abroad, and all, depending upon the locale, necessarily participate in some aspects of third cultural life as part of their encounters with local bureaucracies, foreign embassies, Peace Corps personnel, and missionaries. My Ethiopian experience was atypical in that, along with my fieldwork in traditional Ethiopian society and rather conventional contact with the official face of the third culture, I further entered into the closely bounded world of the permanent expatriate community. Through marriage I became part of one of its prominent subgroups, a Sephardic Jewish community originally from Aden.

While attention has been given in sociological and anthropological literature to the distinctive cultural patterns of some communities within the third culture (Shack and Skinner 1979), only rarely do ethnographers write about the third culture in relation to their own research experience (Weidman [1970]1986: 247).

Ethnographers have not often discussed or acknowledged their own relationship to the third culture; they have in fact avoided such contact, because of the often privileged economic status of third culture members, and because of the historical relationship of many of these communities to a colonial past. Yet what may on the surface appear to be a community more similar to the Western fieldworker's than that of the host country is in reality a special and multifaceted category of social life and experience.

In the case of Ethiopia just before the revolution, the third culture was unusually large and heterogeneous. This was partly due to historical factors that distinguished the Ethiopian experience from that of most of the rest of Africa. In contrast to the frequent resentment of and conflict with stranger communities in postcolonial Africa, "tolerance and indifference, and the absence of overt forms of hostility, for the most part characterize the attitudes of the Ethiopians toward strangers, whatever the strangers' racial or ethnic origins or religious leanings. Historical fact reinforced the centuries-old conviction of the Ethiopians that they have never been deprived of power, even to a relative extent, by immigrant groups, either in the distant past or under contemporary conditions" (Shack 1979: 44).

As the modern headquarters of numerous international health organizations, the site of one of the largest diplomatic corps in Africa, and the home of the Organization for African Unity, Addis Ababa at the time of my arrival in 1973 sustained a third culture of impressive size and diversity. The members of the third culture were easily identified by dress and housing patterns: most wore Western dress and lived in modern apartment buildings in the center of town or in their own villas in outlying neighborhoods adjacent to the old and new airports, respectively. Language was not in itself a reliable marker of the third culture, nor was race. Many expatriates spoke Amharic, the Ethiopian national language, while many urban Ethiopians spoke English, Italian, and other languages; likewise, so large a number of Ethiopians, Africans, and other people of color were part of the third culture that race was rendered an irrelevant variable. The most telling characteristic of third cultural association, apart from Western and other non-Ethiopian dress, was the presence of an intense multilingualism.

As I became part of the third culture, on what I thought would be a permanent basis, I learned of the complex social and institutional networks linking its expatriate members to each other as well as to many in the Ethiopian aristocracy and professional community. Material and medical needs for all were supplied by special shops and hospitals, while social life centered around a small number of restaurants and social clubs, the latter affiliated with the major hotels. Private schools established by expatriates served both foreigners and Ethiopians. Intensive philanthropic activity was carried out by individuals of all nationalities who participated in various clubs, inevitably segregated by gender.

As I look back on my Ethiopian experience, I note that my closest personal relationships were with expatriates from the third culture and Ethiopians who were themselves involved in this arena and/or who had lived abroad. This was a reality of my field experience, despite my concerted efforts to establish and maintain close relationships with others in the "first culture" of traditional Ethiopian society (Useem, Useem, and Donoghue 1963: 169). I suspect that a Western woman in the field can more easily find a place of personal comfort in the third culture, especially in a country where her gender immediately renders her marginal.

Although my entry into the permanent foreign community initially opened new worlds of experience, the course of the revolution eventually had the effect of limiting my physical mobility, restricting me to the Shelemay compound and, by 1975, constraining my relationships with other Ethiopians. To a greater extent than I would have preferred, then, I experienced life in revolutionary Ethiopia with the Shelemays. But it is equally certain that without them I would never have experienced it at all, since I would have left the country once prospects for continuing village fieldwork were foreclosed in the spring of 1974.

There is also no doubt that as time went by, my most powerful emotional attachment became the one to my husband and his family. The chaos all around us most certainly heightened, in our case, the bonding process that necessarily takes place during the early years of a marriage. As the revolution proceeded, I came to realize while writing this book, my perspective shifted to reflect my increasing involvement with and attachment to members of the third culture.

For a child of the sixties who often spoke of revolutions, experiencing a real one provided a sobering initiation into life as well as a bewildering setting in which to carry out a scholarly enterprise. My response to Ethiopian political events was shaped in basic ways by my enculturation as an American, particularly one who came of age during an era of intense political ferment; I have often speculated that the impact of the civil rights movement during my formative years must have subtly influenced my choice of an African field site. But in the end my religious background and gender proved to be the most important variables in all dimensions of my Ethiopian experience.

I have earlier acknowledged that the provocative Jewish component in Ethiopian culture was a powerful force in my initial attraction to Ethiopian studies (Shelemay [1986]1989: 1). My own familiarity with Jewish tradition provided an entry into a central theme of Ethiopian history and cultural life.

I came from a family that could be characterized as deeply involved in the Jewish community while not particularly observant of Jewish religious law. Although I certainly identified myself as a Jew, I always felt myself to have been shaped much more firmly by secular American values and experiences. For this reason I perhaps did not anticipate the extent to which I would be greeted as a religious insider in Ethiopia, and the manner in which I would have to reshape constantly my own identity and behavior to accommodate others' expectations. The communities and individuals to whom I related closely—the Ethiopian Jews, the Sephardic Jews from Aden, and the clergy of the Judaized Ethiopian church—each saw themselves as living a tradition of which I was in some way a part. Aside from the behavioral implications of these shifting associations, I could not have anticipated the emotional impact of encountering each of these communities in crisis, nor the manner in which I would come to share their upheaval.

If I were always aware of my Jewish identity, as an adult my more immediate philosophical and political orientation was as a feminist. Long after returning from the field, I was interested to read Carolyn Heilbrun's observation that having been a Jew rendered her an outsider, and as a result, permitted her to be a feminist (1979: 20). I suspect that the same may have been true of me and that this may account for the highly charged moments that resulted when these two self-images came into conflict. I might also wish to add ethnomusicologist as a third, closely linked identity, since the ethnomusicologist is always the professional outsider and, very frequently, a woman. I now wonder if my past ability to restrict my voice as a writer to that of the ethnomusicologist may not have arisen from the fact that this identity, at least for me, in part subsumed the others.

During the course of writing this book I have come to realize how much of my Ethiopian experience was shaped by the fact that I am a woman. During my preparation for the field I was deeply influenced by others' discussions of their field experiences, particularly those written by women (Wax 1971). I vividly remember reading Peggy Golde's *Women in the Field* (1970) as a graduate student and having a flash of recognition when encountering her introductory summary of "recurring themes" in the female research process. Although I had yet to go to Ethiopia, I had already experienced the first stage, which Golde termed "protection": "an assessment of the vulnerability of the woman seen in terms of relative physical weakness, lesser resourcefulness in confronting unforeseen hazards, or openess to physical attack" (Golde [1970]1986: 5). As I struggled to convince skeptical advisors that I could successfully carry out fieldwork with male priests in rural Ethiopia, an awareness that other women had overcome similar resistance was of great help. This knowledge, along with the moral support of my parents and the timely offer of a fellowship from the National Foundation for Jewish Culture, was critical in helping me circumvent protective maneuvers that ranged from active discouragement to patronization to well-intentioned concern. I carried Elenore Smith Bowen's *Return to Laughter* ([1954] 1964) with me to Ethiopia in 1973. Seventeen years later, well into my own academic career, I understand better the academic politics that led Laura Bohannan both to fictionalize her account of the fieldwork experience and to adopt a pseudonym. But when reading *Return to Laughter* in northern Ethiopia during the fall of 1973, I was as yet unaware of these issues and was simply absorbed in the story it told. It was a symbol of what I too could do as a woman, and a lesson in the way experience could empower me to "reinvent" my own life (Heilbrun 1988: 31).

Through the years of my Ethiopian fieldwork, and since then in other professional contexts, I have often been aware of the way in which gender has shaped the topics I have studied, influenced my research strategies, and colored the resulting interpretations. Until now, however, I have been reluctant to acknowledge fully this impact, both for its positive and negative aspects, and to take the further step of allowing it to emerge in my writing.

I have continued to follow with interest the writings of those who have discussed ethnographic experience from the female perspective (Cesara 1982; Abu-Lughod 1986; Doubleday [1988] 1990). These writings have contributed to the broader trend, now so topical in the social sciences, toward reflexive representations of the field experience (Rabinow 1977; Crapanzano 1980; Marcus and Fisher 1986). Some female ethnographers have crossed over the conventional boundaries of genre (Briggs 1970; Cesara 1982; Shostak 1981) to express themselves in a prose style that may well constitute a "women's language" (Showalter 1982: 20–23). Perhaps no more striking example exists than in a recent work by anthropologist Edith Turner, who discusses her own experiment with ethnographic form and content in powerful female imagery: "Is the book, then, a novel, a memoir, or an anthropological account? I would like to call it advocacy anthropology in the female style, that is, speaking on behalf of a culture as a lover or a mother. I decided to use all the observations, knowledge, and field material that I and Vic had collected, and form them—these actual facts of fieldwork, not imaginary material—into a coherent story, adding my own blood of motherhood, as it were, to feed the embryo so that it might grow in its own true way" (1987: x).

I have chosen to write my book in a narrative style similar to that of many women before me. I found myself uncomfortable with using what might be termed postmodern literary devices or incorporating an explicit critical apparatus that would interrupt the flow of the text. Both, I concluded, would have necessitated a separation of self and subject I was trying to avoid. I have therefore tried to write this book in my own voice, to set forth clearly the ways the situations I found myself in, as well as my own predilections and responses, helped shaped my course of scholarly action and conclusions. I leave it to the reader to critique my biases and shortcomings, both very much in evidence in the following pages. Whatever evaluation the reader will make, I hope that this book will also be read as a deeply felt remembrance of a particular time, people, and place.

A Note on the Transliteration of Foreign Words

Names and terms in Amharic and Ge'ez have been spelled to facilitate their pronunciation by readers. For this reason, the transliteration is not strictly consistent and all diacritical markings are omitted. Only the singular forms of Ge'ez and Amharic nouns cited are used in the text, reflecting the Ethiopian practice of omitting plural markers. Individuals will be referred to by their first names, following Ethiopian custom.

A SONG OF LONGING

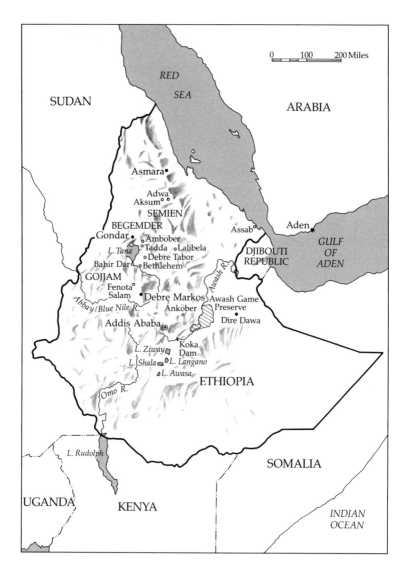

MAP OF ETHIOPIA

1

THE SCHOLAR'S WORLD

The blue Fiat taxi rattled its way down the road leading from Bole International Airport into the city. It was dawn one overcast August day and a mist hung on the eucalyptus trees shadowing the pitted, blacktopped avenue. White-cloaked figures seemed to slip by silently along the shoulders of the road, only their eyes exposed to the morning air full with the smell of burning wood. A few led donkeys loaded with lumpy parcels strapped precariously to their backs. Small bungalows were almost hidden from view behind low stone walls topped with wrought-iron fences, but down side lanes one could glimpse dilapidated tin-roofed huts with smoke curling upward from the eaves. Occasionally, a multistory building of beige stone flanked the road-way.

After curving around a large circle dominated by high-rise buildings, the taxi turned on to a wide boulevard and pulled to the curb. Over a clunking sound made by the idling engine, the driver turned and asked in broken English, "Wabe Shabelle Hotel, is o.k. for you?"

"Yes, thank you," I answered, in equally tentative Amharic. I had arrived in Ethiopia.

From the windows of my hotel room, Addis Ababa appeared an incongruous mixture of old and new. People, vehicles of all shapes and vintages, and donkeys milled about in the streets. Scattered high-rise buildings intermingled with stone-walled compounds enclosing modern villas and workshops. Yet immediately adjacent to these stood clusters of huts. The sea of corrugated tin roofs that sheltered all this architectural hodgepodge glinted in the morning sun. Looking north one could see, perched high on the hill, the older part of the city, its many imposing buildings including the red-roofed palace built for Emperor Menelik II in the late nineteenth century.

My Ethiopian journey had begun quite by accident three years earlier on a crisp fall afternoon in Ann Arbor, Michigan. A first-term graduate student in musicology, I attended one day as usual a required medieval music class, where the study of European Christian chant dominated the agenda. Yet on this day, in a gesture both ecumenical and cross-cultural, the professor played a recording of Ethiopian Falasha liturgical music.

A surprising amount had been written about the people sometimes called the "black Jews of Ethiopia," from descriptions left by European explorers and missionaries of the eighteenth and nineteenth centuries, to twentieth-century linguistic and literary studies. Most emphasized their perpetuation of Jewish traditions, especially the Saturday Sabbath, and the fact that they had maintained a distinctive religious identity as Beta Israel, "House of Israel," within an Orthodox Christian country. Most of what I read also presented these people as anomalies, remnants of Jewish tradition somehow lost in Ethiopia.

But I had been struck by the absence of information concerning Falasha liturgical prayer and music, and soon found out that there was a field of study called ethnomusicology where research of this kind might be done. Ethnomusicologists study music in and as culture, and like anthropologists are expected to undertake a period of independent research called fieldwork, living among the musicians whose traditions they hope to document and interpret. By the end of my first semester in graduate school I knew that I wanted to be an ethnomusicologist and that I wanted to study the Falasha. Simultaneously my interests led me more generally into Ethiopian cultural studies, about which I had become increasingly curious.

Much of what I read described Ethiopia as almost biblical in ethos, a country closely tied to a proud past. Archaeological remains at the early Ethiopian capital, Aksum, testify to the scope of its kingdom, which by the second and third centuries ruled the northern highlands and was in contact with peoples from the Nile Valley to southern Arabia. The conversion of the Emperor Ezana to Christianity in the fourth century established a church that both nurtured a uniquely Judaized form of Christianity and influenced all aspects of Ethiopian cultural, economic, and political life.

Knowledge of the history of Ethiopia until the thirteenth century remains cloudy because so few indigenous historical sources survive. The Aksumite empire apparently declined and was displaced by new rulers who came to power in the tenth century. Of the kings of the subsequent Zagwe dynasty, who assumed the throne in the early twelfth century, we know most about Emperor Lalibela. He constructed the famous rock churches at Roha around the year 1200, designating them the "New Jerusalem" in Ethiopia.

The year 1270 marked the establishment of the "Solomonic dynasty," a lineage of emperors that was to maintain its power with only brief interruptions until 1974. These emperors claimed descent from King Solomon through his son, Menelik, said to have been conceived during the king's famous liaison with the Queen of Sheba. The Ethiopian national epic, the *Kebra Nagast*, records that Menelik stole the Ark of the Covenant from Solomon's Temple in Jerusalem during a visit to his father and brought it back with him to Ethiopia. The Solomonic emperors, as heads of church and state, expanded the borders of their empire while managing a series of internal religious disputes. Several centuries of growth were halted early in the sixteenth century by a Muslim invasion from the south that devastated everything in its path. Only with the help of the Portuguese did Ethiopia manage to defeat the invaders in 1541 and salvage an empire in ruins. Ethiopian regeneration took nearly a century, culminating in the establishment of a new capital at Gondar in the northwest highlands.

The Gondar period was a time of military consolidation and cultural creativity, with a flowering of literature, architecture, and music. By 1769, however, the authority of the Gondar emperors had become so compromised by the power of local princes that they effectively lost control of the state. Only with the coronation of Emperor Theodore in 1855 did the monarchy again regain its authority. A series of new, more international concerns lay ahead. A conflict culminating in a brief British invasion led to Theodore's suicide, while his successor, King John, was confronted by military challenges from Egypt. Ethiopia also struggled against colonialism, and John's successor, Emperor Menelik, won a famous battle against the Italians at Adwa. Although Ethiopia retained her independence, in the end the crown could not prevent the establishment of a permanent Italian presence in Eritrea. This marked the beginning of a tense relationship with Italy that culminated in its brief occupation of all of Ethiopia in the late 1930s.

In the 1880s, Menelik established his seat of power at Addis Ababa, which remains the modern capital. The twentieth century saw Ethiopia stake out a distinctive political course under the guidance of Ras Tafari, who became regent in 1916 and took the name Haile Selassie upon his coronation in 1930.

This national drama replete with elements of faith and intrigue has all been enacted within a stunning landscape. At its center is a rugged highland plateau bisected by the Rift Valley and studded to the north with peaks reaching 14,000 feet. Despite the brief interludes of foreign contact and conquest the Ethiopians have remained fiercely independent, perhaps encouraged by this unforgiving terrain.

If the biblical image was often invoked to describe the past, modern Ethiopia was synonymous with Emperor Haile Selassie I. His 1936 appearance in Geneva before the League of Nations to protest the Italian invasion had left the indelible impression of a courageous ruler. Much of the emperor's energy had been devoted to establishing the economic and political infrastructure of a modern state, with particularly ambitious efforts in the areas of health care and education. After over fifty years of absolute rule the emperor had become a symbol to much of the Western world of Christian faith and modernity in an increasingly unstable Africa.

While Ethiopia fitted my notion of a fine place to do fieldwork, the idea met with considerable resistance from others. One of my musicology professors, hearing of my intention to study Ethiopian music, remarked that "I would soon get over it," giving me the sense that she considered ethnomusicology to be an infection from which I would certainly recover. During the oral examination at which my dissertation topic was approved one committee member could not resist asking me if the Falasha were something one ate for dessert.

My parents, however, were enthusiastic, having seen me off many times before to various points abroad. Accustomed to my taste for cross-cultural adventure, they supported my plans in every possible way. They collected all information about Ethiopia that came their way and sent me a clipping from the Jewish Press that alerted me to the fellowship that eventually supported my research. My mother helped me sort out what I might need of personal effects in the field, accompanying me on a round of medical appointments to make sure all was in order before I left. Only once did she indicate the slightest hesitation about my plans, a moment neither of us shall ever forget.

We had long before established a small ritual of packing together before my trips. Inevitably, as we arranged the last items in the suitcase and tried to recall what we might have left out, mother would look at me solemnly. "Well," she would remark, "it's not the wilds of Africa you know. If you forget something, you can get it there." In May 1973, while I was briefly at our Texas home preparing for my departure to Ethiopia later that summer, mother had gotten as far as "Well, it's not the wilds,"—and then burst into tears. Indeed, it was the wilds of Africa at last.

Despite our jokes about the wilds, or the myths of biblical Ethiopia, that first day it was modern Africa I encountered. As I wandered in and out of small shops along streets near the hotel, shopkeepers encouraged my attempts at Amharic conversation before diplomatically letting me know that they also spoke English. Storefronts were crowded with Ethiopian souvenirs—graceful birds carved of cow horn, soft cloth dolls in traditional Ethiopian dresses, silver crosses, cartoon-like representations of the story of Solomon and Sheba painted on parchment—all displayed for tourists. At one shop I saw Ethiopian goldwork at prices that took my breath away. At another, I admired handmade Ethiopian imperial capes of embroidered velvet.

Amid these elegant stores were also butcher shops with fly-specked carcasses hanging unrefrigerated from iron hooks. Kiosks sold matches, odds and ends, and cigarettes, single or by the pack. There were bars where one could stop for a drink or a meal; or, if one were so inclined, one could order drinks while sitting in a car at the curb. Many of these shops carried the names of their Italian owners, part of the sizeable Italian community that had remained in Ethiopia after the occupation.

Some sights shocked immediately: there were women bent like beasts of burden under unwieldy bundles of wood, children running about clad only in soiled rags, lepers with missing limbs begging on every corner. A pungent smell pervaded the air, a mixture of eucalyptus wood and cow dung burning within the scattered huts. This combined with an acrid odor I would learn later was *berbere,* the fiery red pepper mixed from dozens of spices that is added to Ethiopian food. For twenty-four hours I looked, listened, and smelled, my pace slowing, my apprehensions dissolving as I encountered a series of friendly faces.

The next morning I gathered my things and prepared to enter the scholar's world. Carol, a husky, blond American anthropologist soon to leave the country after a year studying the lives of women in a distant Ethiopian province, came to my hotel to guide me to the house where she and other visiting researchers boarded. For the newcomer, finding one's way in urban Ethiopia is quite a challenge. Though some streets do have names they are often unmarked, and buildings are not numbered. Any invitation is invariably tendered with a map, lengthy verbal description of landmarks and peculiarities of buildings, or preferably both.

Carol and I made our way across the city. We climbed, with my pack and recording equipment, on and off large red buses of the Ambassa (Lion) Bus Company. Painted on the side of each bus was, predictably, the figure of a lion, the imperial emblem of the emperor known as the Lion of Judah because of his Solomonic descent.

On closer inspection, the modern high-rises and tin-roofed shacks seemed defiant in their contrast. The people too seemed caught between worlds: into modern buildings walked men in the traditional white jodhpurs and *shamma*, a cotton, toga-like garment, alongside others in Western suits and ties.

There were signs of the emperor everywhere. We came to a roundabout where a large stone sculpture stood, depicting a stylized lion haughtily turning to stare into the distance, wearing a large crown topped with a cross. How long would the eighty-one-year-old emperor wear his crown and continue to exercise absolute power? Exiled from Ethiopia during the Italian occupation of his country, he had returned triumphantly in 1941 and restored stability. Once, when he was away on a state trip in 1960, there had been an attempt to unseat him and to replace him with the crown prince. Then, too, Haile Selassie had returned to his country and regained his power. Thirteen years later he remained in absolute control, a figure every bit as formidable as the stone Lion of Judah in the square. But at the same time there lingered the unanswerable question: What will happen when the emperor is gone? The succession of the crown prince had been compromised by the 1960 attempted coup, and the popular younger son had tragically died in a plane crash a few years later. Despite the uncertainty there was a complacent feeling, almost a blind faith that the legacy of this monarch would sustain his country through whatever transition lay ahead.

We continued up a steep boulevard and passed the striking circular building that housed the Commercial Bank of Ethiopia. Above us at the top of the hill sat the city hall. On a higher ridge nearby stood the imposing Saint George Church, its golden dome glinting in the distance. It was at this church that Haile Selassie had been crowned emperor of Ethiopia so many years before.

The bus struggled up the steep road, belching acrid black smoke, while the cars wheezed their way up in low gear. At a large circle inexplicably called Tewodros Square, we got off the bus and crossed the street to a ramshackle house with a red corrugated iron roof, pale green walls with flaking paint, and a rickety green picket fence. A few untrimmed rose bushes, heavy with fresh leaves and buds after the long rainy season, dotted the yard. As we entered the compound a loud snore greeted us from the hut alongside the gate. "It's only the *zabanya*," Carol reassured me; this was my introduction to the vigilance typical of these round-the-clock guards charged with securing urban homes.

The house belonged to Faye, a middle-aged English teacher who had left England in search of a job and found one in Ethiopia. Eccentric and inventive, she took in boarders both for the diversion they offered on quiet, rainy evenings and for the boost they provided to her modest income.

It was a pleasant enough house, with several bedrooms available to visitors in need of a cheap and decent place to stay. With the cook, the grizzled guard, and three Ethiopian students living in and available for odd jobs, Faye's provided a comfortable base, particularly if one were prepared to overlook the crumbling mud-and-wattle walls of the kitchen and the unreliable plumbing. Such inconveniences were more than balanced by the somewhat zany atmosphere and modest, if bizarre, amusements. While sitting quietly in the living room on the worn sofa or nearby armchair, the sharp eye could detect subtle movements in the black-and-white colubus monkey rug, the constant dance of its resident fleas. Anyone entering the house was required to sign a visitor's book despite the number of previous visits, a custom well known to all and an unfailing source of hilarity anytime Faye happened to be out of earshot.

A remarkable array of individuals turned up most evenings, visiting scholars, longtime expatriate residents of the capital, Ethiopian friends of those who were or had once been residents at Faye's. All sat around, drinking from bottles they brought with them or whatever happened to be available, weaving their own Ethiopian tales, or listening to recordings of Ethiopian music on a raspy cassette tape recorder, often humming along.

All that morning the ringing of church bells had signaled a celebration. I was told that the day marked the end of a three-week fast period. After settling into my small and utilitarian room, with its single iron bed and wooden bureau, I asked one of the young students of the household, Zemede, to accompany me to church for my first view of the festivities.

A holiday atmosphere prevailed outside a church named for the archangel Gabriel. People crowded around the numerous makeshift stands that sold raisins, nuts, and jewelry. The Gabriel Church, like most others in highland Ethiopia, is built in the round. Divided into three concentric chambers, the innermost section, the "Holy of Holies," houses the *tabot*, a replica of the Ark of the Covenant. Only the priests—or the Ethiopian emperor—are allowed to enter this sacred space. With the middle chamber of the church used primarily by the clergy, men and women flow in and out of the large outermost chamber where the hymnary is performed by musicians. In Ethiopian Christian tradition the most elaborate music takes place before the Mass, when a highly trained group of men called *debtera* chants long poetic texts with instrumental accompaniment.

According to well-established tradition, the women would enter a separate door on the south side of the church. When I paused, unsure of which way to go, Zemede pushed me forward with the men. Embarrassed, I turned to move back toward the women but was stopped by a tall musician who handed me a *meqwamiya*, the traditional staff used for support during long hours of prayer. He led me through the crowd inside the door to a spot in the first row among the men, a development that at first startled and further embarrassed me, but that I would later realize characterized my ambiguous status as a foreign woman in the field.

My initial discomfort with this preferential treatment faded into excitement as I watched the ritual I otherwise would not have been able to see from the distant women's section. In front of me were two parallel lines of *debtera* in white gowns and turbans, facing each other. Four drummers, one positioned at the end of each row, beat the large kettledrums, the *kebaro*, each drum covered with a bright pink flowered cloth held in place by the leather thongs that also secured both drum heads. The drummers set a steady rhythm that slowly accelerated, while each of the other *debtera* held in his right hand a sistrum, a delicate silver rattle with a wooden handle. As these musicians shook their sistra in unison, a gentle tinkling sound merged with the strong, booming voice of the *kebaro*.

The gentle patterns of the drums and sistra continued, accompanying the nasal, fluid chant. Then, suddenly, the speed of the drumming increased dramatically and the musicians put down their sistra and prayer staffs. As they clapped their hands and started to sway, the beat became faster still and the musicians jumped several times, the two parallel lines melding into a circle. Their faces looked exultant as they threw their bodies from side to side. Then, as abruptly as it began, the beat subsided, the musicians once again reclaimed their sistra and prayer staffs, and resumed their places in line. We remained for the rest of the service, leaving only after the musicians completed their singing in preparation for the performance of the Mass by the priests.

The following days in Addis Ababa were marked by a flurry of activity. Scholars wishing to carry out research in Ethiopia were first required to obtain the approval of the Institute of Ethiopian Studies at the Haile Selassie I University. Founded in 1961 under imperial charter, the university occupied the buildings and grounds that had once been the palace of Emperor Haile Selassie. One entered through wide iron gates bearing the imperial initials into grounds covered with a luxuriant growth of bougainvillea and other flowering shrubs. The ubiquitous eucalyptus trees, commonly known as *baher zaf*, the overseas trees, had been introduced to Ethiopia by the British in the early twentieth century. Here they shaded landscaped walkways that led to the buildings dotting the still-elegant grounds.

Inside the Institute, wood-paneled stairs led up to a reading room filled with books about Ethiopia. A museum with Ethiopian paintings, artifacts, and musical instruments was tucked away in an adjacent room, with the offices of the director and staff just across a lobby.

One always wondered what other treasures the former palace held. On a rare occasion when I was allowed to move beyond the library confines, I caught a glimpse of what had once been one of the palace toilets. Only a porcelain bathtub on stubby, curved legs remained of the original fixtures. The rest of the white-tiled room was filled with hanging gongs, small knobbed pots in wooden holders, and innumerable metal-keyed instruments, the residue of an Indonesian gamelan that must once have been a state gift to the emperor.

The Institute of Ethiopian Studies was the lifeline of the foreign scholar, both institutional home and protector. Only through the Institute could one receive permission to enter the country. Once a scholar had been accepted, the Institute helped smooth the rough edges of Ethiopian bureaucracy, arranging the residency visa and necessary letters of introduction to officials of the region where the individual planned to work. The usual path took one from the Institute, where initial residency papers were prepared and approved, to the offices of immigration, and finally to the Foreign Ministry, where the ultimate authority rested. The procedure could take a few days or a few months, and some unlucky souls, perhaps having selected a controversial subject or place, or being just unfortunate, ended up spending most of their fellowship period trying to get an answer from the Foreign Ministry.

My visa procedure was completed expeditiously. The official at the Foreign Ministry who processed my papers at first told me to come back after a week, at which I expressed surprise and politely asked if the papers might not be ready sooner. "Ah, you're a clever one," he murmured in Amharic with a faint smile. He would have my papers ready the following day, he said, and, indeed, they were waiting for me the next afternoon.

My personal possessions, soon to arrive by air, were a source of greater anxiety. They included everything from magnetic tapes to cosmetics and an assortment of remedies for potential medical emergencies, including a snake-bite kit complete with tourniquet and incision knives.

Little did I know that there are hardly any snakes to be found in the higher elevations of Ethiopia where I planned to do my research. But somewhere in the many books I had read about field-work the novice was advised to be prepared for all eventualities, even snakes, and I had dutifully included the kit.

In the few days since my arrival in the country I had been told stories of heartless customs officials who would levy exhorbitant taxes on the possessions of scholars or, worse still, would confiscate items altogether. Taking no chances I went to the airport armed with a letter from the Institute explaining my project, accompanied by one of the director's assistants as well as a driver.

We entered the customs building and were shown to the office of a short official with aquiline features. He looked at me closely, examined the shipping papers before him, and asked questions about my plans. Why did I have so many tapes? Didn't I know that they had a very high resale value? I explained that I needed enough both to make original recordings and to leave copies in Ethiopia.

After a few more questions, he initialed the forms and pushed his chair back from his desk. "If your driver will come around to the door, he can load your trunk in the car," he told me. "By the way," he continued with a broad smile, "my wife and I have a very good friend who is in the Peace Corps and she will be coming to our house for dinner next week. Would you like to join us?" Relieved by the speed with which the matter was concluded and at the same time surprised and very pleased by the spontaneous invitation, I hastily accepted.

With papers and possessions now in hand I had in fact completed the major preparations for my trip to Gondar, the small northwestern town that had once been the capital of the empire. I planned to leave Addis Ababa in mid-September, arriving in time to witness the major Beta Israel holidays that would begin later that month.

Now that the visa and customs procedures were unexpectedly out of the way, I had several extra weeks to polish my Amharic, explore the capital, and begin to feel more at home. I arranged to take private lessons in Addis Ababa with a highly recommended tutor. Every day I went to the university for a lesson with Sinait, a young aspiring social worker who supported herself by tutoring visiting scholars like myself.

The large and friendly group of visiting scholars provided company and reassurance during those early weeks, most often meeting at a fast-food storefront for the local version of a hamburger. But it was my friend Tesemma, the first Ethiopian I had met in the United States, who was to introduce me to traditional Ethiopian cuisine.

Just as with Ethiopian music, I had encountered Tesemma by chance. I had been reading a book about Ethiopia while riding across Ann Arbor on a University of Michigan bus and glanced up to see a man across the aisle who looked just like a picture on the page before me.

"Are you Ethiopian?" I blurted out, immediately embarrassed.

"Yes," replied Tesemma. "How did you know?" Sheepishly, I held up my book and explained that I was planning to study Ethiopian music.

A slim man with finely chiseled features, Tesemma was completing his dissertation in chemistry. In the months that followed he became my Amharic tutor and friend. Often, Tesemma would invite me to eat Ethiopian food at the house he shared with two other Ethiopian students.

"In Ethiopia I don't do the cooking," he warned me several times. "But there I'll take you to some good restaurants I know."

Often Ethiopian restaurants are housed in modest buildings that a newcomer without a knowing guide might not enter. Inside a large room are scattered traditional Ethiopian *mesob*, large hourglass-shaped baskets that serve as tables when their tops are removed. Seats are wooden stools barely ten inches high upon which one squats. The walls are decorated with round, black-and-white colubus monkey rugs. Sometimes there is a musician playing traditional Ethiopian songs. The national dish consists of a flat pancake-like bread called *injera*, upon which is ladeled various peppery stews of vegetables, chicken, and meat mixed with a few hard-boiled eggs. The food is eaten by tearing pieces of the *injera* and scooping up the stew. The first time Tesemma tried to insert an entire egg into my mouth, I was startled and didn't know how to react. Only afterward did he explain that to offer a choice morsel is a traditional way to indicate one's friendship and respect.

In those first weeks I met officials of the Institute of Ethiopian Studies and the university, many of whom offered hospitality. The Institute was directed by Richard Pankhurst, the son of one of the three daughters of the famous family of British suffragettes. The Pankhurst association with Ethiopia had begun during the Italian occupation in the late 1930s, when Richard's mother, Sylvia, befriended Emperor Haile Selassie during his years of exile in England. Afterward, Sylvia spent long periods of time in Ethiopia and penned a thick volume about its cultural history. Richard was equally attached to the country and became a scholar, documenting Ethiopian economic and social life and assuming the management of the Institute, which supported such studies. I enjoyed a leisurely lunch at the Pankhurst home. We chatted about American feminism, a subject of great interest to Richard's wife, Rita, who headed the university library. All the while, I kept a nervous eye on their friendly Great Dane.

All long-term residents in Ethiopia were asked to register at their own embassies so that there would be some record of their whereabouts in case of an emergency. Early in my stay, I stopped by and signed in at the U.S. Embassy, which occupied a large and beautifully landscaped compound just up the hill from the university, next door to the imposing residence of the crown prince.

That same day I also decided on impulse to stop by the Israeli Embassy. There I hoped to meet several officials whose names had been given to me by friends in Jerusalem, where I had lived the previous year studying Ethiopian languages. I made the long trip by bus out to Bishoftu Road, then walked the last half-mile or so along the muddy road on the outskirts of the city to where the Israeli Embassy occupied a well-guarded compound. After several cordial conversations and a number of cups of coffee, I walked out through the embassy parking lot, where I noticed that the same woman who had greeted me on my way in was still sitting in her Land Rover. "Would you like a ride back to the center of town?" she called out. With an emphatic nod and a sigh of relief, I climbed in, thrilled to avoid a certain splashing from passing cars. This was my first encounter with Marian Robinson.

Marian had accompanied her husband, Bill, to Ethiopia. He was a veterinarian on temporary assignment with an American research unit established to study primates. Bill mainly worked in the capital but often traveled down to a rough camp set up for research purposes in the Awash game park, several hours' drive to the southeast.

Marian had long brown hair that she sometimes wore braided, making her look every bit the Georgia farm girl she once had been. A former elementary school teacher, she had been delighted to leave teaching for an assignment abroad. The Robinsons lived in an area of the capital, near the old airport, that had become something like an American colony, so heavily was it populated by American diplomats and officials in Ethiopia on short-term contracts. As did many wives in the foreign community, Marian spent her time organizing their personal lives and doing various good works, volunteering through the American Women's Club for local causes ranging from Ethiopian orphans to area hospitals.

"Are you waiting for someone?" I asked.

"It's a rather long story," Marian replied.

I was to learn that Marian and Bill were a childless couple who frequently shared their home and kindness with others who crossed their path. That particular day Marian was waiting for her latest house guest, one Mrs. Rosen, who had insisted that she must meet the Israeli ambassador to Ethiopia.

Mrs. Rosen did not know the Israeli ambassador, nor did she have an appointment. She was a plump, energetic Jewish woman of about sixty who along with her husband ran a women's clothing store in New York City. Her daughter Joyce, a doctoral student at a major American university, had come to Ethiopia a few months earlier to investigate possibilities for primate research. Joyce had quickly made contact with Bill and the Awash project, and decided to stay on for some months to gather data for her dissertation. She had informed her parents of her plans, reassuring them that their only daughter was safe and in good company.

Mrs. Rosen always waited anxiously for her daughter's regular weekly letter. One week no letter arrived, not a great surprise to anyone familiar with the vagaries of international mail, let alone the circuitous route a letter must travel from southern Ethiopia to New York. After waiting three days, Mrs. Rosen cabled Joyce in Addis Ababa, but of course received no response since Joyce was then in the isolated research camp set up next to the Awash falls. After two more days had passed, filled with unanswered cables and telephone calls, Mrs. Rosen got on a plane and flew to Addis Ababa. Locating the headquarters of the primate research unit, she met Bill Robinson, who took her home, reassuring her that Joyce was just fine.

Still not satisfied, Mrs. Rosen had insisted on seeing Joyce herself. Bill drove her down the next day. Late that afternoon, Joyce Rosen returned to her canvas tent in the Awash game park after a hard day tagging monkeys to find her feisty, opinionated mother sound asleep on her cot.

I was still convulsed from Marian's story when Mrs. Rosen emerged from the embassy and climbed into the car. Yes, she had met the ambassador, who had evidently decided it would be easier to greet this determined coreligionist from New York than to continue to have his aide make polite excuses.

We drove back to the city, stopping for a coffee at the Masqal Rendezvous, a small restaurant that served a miscellaneous array of American and European dishes. I told the two about my own plans to head north in several weeks. I regaled them at some length with stories about life at Faye's, which in fact had become somewhat lonely with the recent departure of Carol and Faye's own impending home leave to London. I was particularly unsure how to handle the enthusiastic friendship of one of the young male Ethiopian students, who had taken to entering my room without knocking.

"Why don't you come out and stay with us?" offered Marian. "We have two extra bedrooms and you can catch a ride to the university with me or one of our neighbors most days. If no one is going, you can always flag down a taxi." Astonished at the offer, I gratefully accepted, giving her the usual detailed instructions to Faye's house, where she would pick me up later in the week.

Bill and Marian's house was a modern stone bungalow with a tiled roof. The spacious living and dining area adjoined a new, fully furnished, American-style kitchen. The furniture supplied by the research unit was attractive, and the Robinson's newly acquired Ethiopian carpets and paintings lent a local flavor. I was startled by this transplanted American life-style, my shock complete when I opened the refrigerator to find Borden's chocolate milk and Kraft cheese, flown in by air to the U.S. Army's PX.

Although Marian and Bill enjoyed comforts available to members of the official American community, they were very interested in Ethiopian life. Marian had learned to make the *injera*, as well as the local chicken stew, *doro wat*, and served both at dinner at least once a week. She and Bill knew the capital well, and took me on my first tour of the enormous sprawling market, the Mercato, believed to be the largest in Africa.

On many weekends the Robinsons would toss supplies into their Land Rover and head off for an American-run camping ground adjacent to Lake Langano, one of the large lakes of the Rift Valley that stretches to the south of the capital. As one descends from the Shoan plateau, wide open plains dotted with acacia trees stretch out as far as the eye can see, to the foot of distant volcanic hills.

The lakes of the Rift Valley Park Reserve are havens for wildlife. The trees along the lakeshores are alive with baboons, while pelicans, bright pink flamingos, and other water birds cover the shimmering lakes. As we walked along the rough shore, local children approached us, begging for "karamela" (candy), which Bill and Marian had brought along for just such a purpose.

The next day we drove down into an overgrown valley not far from the town of Shashamannee, where everyone in the area appeared to be wending their way along the same rough road to the Sunday market. The narrow track passed through high hills overgrown with thick and luxurious vegetation. Monkeys could be seen high in the trees, swinging from eucalyptus to acacia to euphorbia. As we descended, the colors of bright blooming poinsettia trees and the rich green of vines gave the valley the appearance of a tropical rain forest. We overtook several low horse-drawn carts that pulled aside to let us pass, and everywhere we were greeted with cries of "*ferenj*" (foreigner) and requests for karamela.

We parked alongside the market, which was packed with hundreds of Ethiopians. There were Galla women with tightly braided hairstyles, their bare chests partially covered with necklaces of cowrie shells and beads. Some were wearing traditional leather loincloths while others wore wrapped skirts made of hand-woven cotton or imported textiles.

We looked at rows of iron knives for sale, and at the white cotton *shamma* cloth handmade by local weavers. There were all sorts of spices displayed, many of which we could not identify. Bunches of onions and assorted vegetables were arranged in small mounds. Perhaps the most sought-after items were the blocks of salt offered for sale or barter, mined from the distant salt flats of the Danakil desert along the Red Sea coast. We were as much an object of attention as anything at the market, and many gathered around us to examine our clothing and hair.

The weeks with Marian and Bill passed quickly. When another foreign researcher arrived I returned once more to Faye's house at Tewodros Square and made the final preparations for my departure to Gondar. I had been living almost exclusively in the midst of colleagues and other expatriates in a cosmopolitan setting. Things were soon to change.

2

NORTH TO GONDAR

I had received permission to travel north and to live in Gondar, the modern capital of Begemder-Semien Province and one-time capital of the empire. From there I planned to travel to Beta Israel villages in the area.

The trip from Addis Ababa to Gondar could be accomplished most quickly by a two-hour flight in a World War II–vintage Ethiopian Airlines DC-3 that would buck its way north through the often violent downdrafts over the mountains. This was the usual mode of travel for most foreigners and Ethiopians who could afford the airfare. The only other option was to take a two-day bus ride north through the mountainous terrain that lay between the capital and its northern provinces. Although few appeared to speak from personal experience, most friends and colleagues warned against the long, inconvenient trip overland.

But the rains had just ended in early September and the countryside was in bloom with the yellow, daisy-like *Masqal* flowers named after the Ethiopian holiday that marks the beginning of the new year. Another American scholar, Marilyn Heldman, also needed to go north, and we decided to take the bus together.

The Addis Ababa bus station was located at the edge of the city in an open, dusty field. At 5:30 on the morning of our departure, a large number of buses were parked there in a mass of confusion, without any indication of destination or time of departure. Hundreds of people milled about, each trying to find their bus. Finally locating the Gondar bus, we joined a crowd pushing to board with more parcels and luggage than could be accommodated on the rickety roof racks or inside. Whether because of our sex, race, or formidable appearance in khaki-colored, U.S. Army raincoats and hiking boots, we were led to the front of the line and given the first seat behind the driver.

Next to us sat a young Ethiopian man. After looking with interest at a parcel under his feet that periodically shook, we politely asked what was in it. "Just chickens for my relative," he answered, opening the straw cover to expose two nervous-looking chickens whose future certainly included becoming *doro wat*.

Three hours later the bus pulled out of the station and we were on our way. We left the city through a maze of narrow streets that criss-crossed the Mercato, filled with people and heavily laden donkeys snarling the traffic. Here and there were rows of shops and open-air stalls, offering every imaginable item from exotic spices to empty bottles. Finally we made our way out of the market and entered the road leading north.

From the window we could see farmers guiding emaciated bulls pulling single plowshares, preparing their fields for crops of corn and *tef*, an indigenous cereal. Here and there among the plowed fields, delineated one from the other by shrub and cactus fences, were uncultivated areas where herds of cattle and sheep grazed on the newly budding grass. At the edge of each small farm stood a round hut with a thatched conical roof, home to a farmer and his family.

As the route approached the riverbed of the Abbay a couple of hours north of Addis Ababa, the terrain grew more rugged and the climb steeper. Level ground on one side of the road often gave way to a chasm on the other. We threaded our way over a recently constructed bridge that stretched like a ribbon over the gorge, and wound up the mountains on the other side. Sharing raisins and nuts with our neighbor, we were regaled by Ethiopian lyre music blasting loudly over the bus's radio as fields covered with yellow and purple wildflowers rushed past.

But in the mid-afternoon our idyll ended. The bus was flagged down by an irate villager who insisted that the driver had run over his most valuable donkey the last trip through. After an hour of intense negotiation a settlement was reached, the driver rejoined us, and the journey resumed. By now the afternoon was waning, and instead of continuing to the large town along the way where we had hotel reservations for the night, we pulled into a tiny village of which we had never heard. It was named Fenota Salam, which means "road to peace."

Countless villages have sprung up alongside the roads in rural Ethiopia. Little more than a block long, they contain a few mud-and-wattle houses, along with a gas station or small store, and certainly a tavern, the latter usually marked by inverted bottles stuck on the thatched roof. Dusty tracks lead away from the blacktop or dirt highway only to disappear into the landscape within a few hundred feet.

The bus pulled off the road. Barely had it come to a halt when everyone rushed toward the door, each struggling to be the first out. No one had reacted to earlier rest stops with such urgency, and I asked our seatmate, who had turned out to be a schoolteacher making his first trip north as well, what was happening. "I think they are trying to get a space in the hotel," he answered. I looked and saw only a dilapidated whitewashed building with a sagging wooden porch in front. The door was open, but whatever was inside was hidden from view by all the bus passengers trying to push through at once.

"Hotel?" I asked.

"Yes," he answered. "There are probably not enough rooms and everyone is running to make sure he gets one."

We did not run fast enough. A man, nattily dressed in the traditional white jodhpurs, jacket, and *shamma*, could be seen sitting at a desk in the room once the crowd had cleared. He glanced up from his book as I stood before him. "No room," he said.

"What do we do?" I asked, remembering tales of bandits said to prey upon passengers who sleep in the bus as an economy measure. He shrugged and shook his head.

I walked out and stood by the side of the road, everyone's admonitions ringing in my ears. Climbing back into the bus, Marilyn and I discussed our predicament. Even our seatmate had disappeared. Suddenly a young man stuck his head through the open door and motioned for us to follow. Grabbing our belongings, we followed him to a building across the road. On the porch stood several young Ethiopian women wearing faded, Western-style cotton dresses. They took us inside and poured us each a beer. Looking around at the large room flanked by smaller rooms, we realized that we were in the tavern, called a *tedj bet*, which serves as both social club and brothel.

As dusk settled our hostesses showed us to one of the small rooms, nearly filled by a well-used bed promising unnamed diseases. For a while we sat inside with the door open, occasionally stepping out into the main room to see what was going on. This *tedj bet* had no live musician to play tunes on the one-stringed bowed instrument called the *masenqo*, so as evening fell someone played *masenqo* music on a small tape recorder. Business picked up as men from the area stopped by to drink and have a good time. We were clearly the subject of many conversations, and as the crowd became rowdier, we began to feel uncomfortable. After a final visit to a maggot-infested outhouse, accompanied by curious neighborhood children and a snarling dog, we retired to our room and locked the door.

We unpacked peanut butter and jelly sandwiches and fruit juice stashed away for just such an emergency and read aloud Philip Roth's *Our Gang* by candlelight. As the noise outside mounted we consoled ourselves with the fact that there were two of us. At around 9:00 P.M. the music stopped, and we laid down upon the flea-ridden bed fully dressed in our hooded raincoats and hiking boots, small utility knives open at our sides.

"Do you think we're overreacting?" asked Marilyn, not entirely rhetorically. We had a hearty laugh, put our knives away, and drifted off to sleep.

At 5:00 A.M. we awoke, hurriedly drank coffee provided by the ladies of the house, left a few Ethiopian dollars in payment, and headed toward the bus. As we walked out the door a group of people laughed and applauded. We knew then that we had been the objects of the local equivalent of a practical joke. We waved, adjusted our packs, and walked across the road to board the bus.

The ride took us across the rest of Gojjam province and into neighboring Begemder-Semien. The rolling landscape gave way to higher mountains with grotesque lava formations. We passed Lake Tana, the source of the Blue Nile, where we could see fishermen along the shore emptying their woven reed boats of the morning's catch. The islands located in the center of the lake were visible in the distance, mysterious and unattainable. Upon them are ancient monasteries filled with illuminated manuscripts and other relics of a Christian tradition over sixteen hundred years old. But a stop would have done us little good—the monasteries are open only to men and we would not have been allowed to enter.

When we arrived in Gondar in the mid-afternoon three Falasha men, notified of our arrival by a member of the community who lived in Addis Ababa, were at the bus station to welcome us. After effusive greetings, I agreed to meet them early the next morning to travel to their village. We had the afternoon to settle in and to begin to investigate what seemed, after Addis Ababa, to be a sleepy provincial capital.

Accommodations in Gondar ranged from a run-down but elegant hotel in a former palace to the ubiquitous *tedj bet*. The American network had prepared us well, however, and we soon arrived with sleeping bags in hand at the home of a Peace Corps volunteer stationed in Gondar. Alex, a Texan who was nearly at the end of his Ethiopian service, relished the thought of returning home to the United States. Given the relative isolation of Gondar, he welcomed visitors.

Anyone who has lived for a few years as a foreigner in an isolated locale understands that with the exoticism of this life-style comes an often grinding loneliness and nearly insatiable desire for things familiar. The few foreigners there on a long-term basis shared a rapport that transcended nationality, age, and background. Above all, they were *ferenj* (literally, "Franks," meaning foreigner, Westerner, white man), and by virtue of this identity were both defined as a group and functioned as a solid support system for one another.

I soon came to know the dozen or so *ferenj* in Gondar. Besides Alex, there was an Englishman who served as superintendent of local schools, an American couple attached to a small public-health college, two high school teachers from Madras who had been in the area for years, two young Frenchmen performing alternative military service, and an American doctor working temporarily at the local hospital. Part of a more extended network were a handful of British men and women who staffed missions in the surrounding area. A visitor to Gondar for more than a few days would likely encounter one of these individuals on the street or in a shop and, after brief preliminaries confirming their shared status, would immediately be invited over for a drink or dinner. The arrival of a new "permanent resident" set off a flurry of social activities designed both to ease the newcomer's adjustment to life in the area and to obtain fresh news of the outside world.

Throughout my stay these newfound friends were sources of companionship, comfort, and advice. Through this socialization process I became more knowledgeable about—and comfortable with—the rather unique social status that the other foreigners and I occupied. Neither natives nor tourists, these long-term foreign residents were immediately noticed by all. Their every action became a potential source of local gossip.

The public eye particularly scrutinized foreign women on their own. In rural Ethiopia a woman's place was at home. The few foreign women who made their way to outlying areas were inevitably the source of considerable attention, and as our own experience had indicated, even the target of an occasional joke. It was also quite easy for a woman to breach local norms and become the object of intense criticism. The *ferenj* quickly filled me in on the most recent scandal concerning a foreign female in Gondar—a young woman briefly in the area to do research had caused great umbrage by visiting *tedj bet* on her own in the evenings and, as rumor had it, sleeping with local men. I was advised to be particularly cautious since I would be scrutinized with my predecessor's reputation in mind.

The *ferenj* network was also a source of gossip and a variety of useful information about the area. Topics of discussion included all available details concerning local politics and noteworthy events. But most frequently discussed were the many ailments dreaded by everyone in the foreign community.

A glance around in any area of Ethiopia left one shaken by the impact of disease in this developing country. On every street corner there were the disfigured and disabled, even in a town like Gondar with a hospital and public-health school. Although treatment was now available for leprosy at a major hospital in the Ethiopian capital, many who suffered from the affliction flocked to provincial centers like Gondar to beg. We all knew that a swim in a stream, or a ride in the famous reed boats on Lake Tana in the event of an inopportune dunking, would result in exposure to bilharzia transmitted by the snails living in the reeds along the banks. Amoebic dysentery was rampant, and frequent warnings were sounded to disinfect vegetables and purify water. It was prudent at lower altitudes to take quinine to prevent malaria. A particularly common and distressing ailment was hepatitis, since it might be contracted from any number of sources and was quite difficult to avoid because of its ubiquity.

These discussions carried with them a certain amount of colorful detail and were part of the larger folklore of the foreign community. A whole repertory of tales existed concerning the effects of tapeworms, usually acquired from the raw meat served as a delicacy by Ethiopians. It amazed me that individuals intrepid enough to spend months or years in rural Ethiopia would continue to discuss the subject with lively interest, until I realized that these conversations operated on a more subtle level to ventilate and resolve the intense conflicts that often arose out of attempts to avoid infection. The offering and acceptance of food are important aspects of traditional Ethiopian hospitality, and those who refuse to partake risk insulting Ethiopian friends.

I remember participating in one particularly heated debate concerning whether or not one could safely eat local food, especially that prepared in the villages. David, the British school superintendent who had lived in the area for many years, and I argued with Bob, the American doctor, that one must respect local custom and, within limits, partake of local cuisine. By eating cooked food and avoiding (often with difficulty) local delicacies such as raw meat and unpasteurized milk, the risk of various infections would be greatly reduced. I would carefully explain, when offered a glass of sour milk as a treat by well-meaning villagers, that milk had always made me sick in America and for this reason I could not drink it in Ethiopia.

David spoke from long experience, I from strong conviction. Bob, however, kept citing the risks involved—describing in graphic detail symptoms of the severe hepatitis that he felt certain we would contract. That particular conversation ended with everyone holding firm to his or her point of view. The next week David came down with hepatitis and had to be flown to Addis Ababa for medical treatment. I weathered my village experience without serious problems, but was constantly aware of the conflict between concerns for health and social expectations in rural Ethiopia.

All this was ahead when we arrived at Alex's house that first day. We quickly dropped off our possessions and set off for the local vice-mayor's office to present my letter of introduction before word of my arrival reached him. In the provinces the presentation of formal letters of introduction is both a legal requirement and a ritual that can insure access and good will. Although Marilyn was just passing through on her way to study church architecture and painting farther north, I planned to be in Gondar for eight to nine months, until the annual rains began.

Leading us into a black-tiled room with a rather spartan desk and chairs, the secretary offered us *bunna*, strong black Ethiopian coffee, while she processed my permission form to live and do research in Begemder-Semien Province. The vice-mayor himself arrived shortly thereafter and, with little fuss, made official my arrival in Gondar.

We spent what was left of that first day walking around the small town nestled in the soft green mountains. Gondar had been the capital of all of Ethiopia in the seventeenth and eighteenth centuries, and grand stone castles built by the emperors during that period still testify to its former greatness. The earliest castle had been built by the emperor Fasiladas in the mid-seventeenth century, along with a separate building that held a bath. Other white and brown stone castles were built by his successors through the mid-eighteenth century, all grouped within the royal compound still encircled by an old stone wall. I looked at the buildings with interest, having read that the Beta Israel were prominent among the masons who helped build these structures with their high towers and parapets ringed with battlements. We sat for a time and watched a family of lions, kept caged on the castle grounds to symbolize the Ethiopian emperors' status as the "Lion of Judah." But then we spotted several cubs roaming freely around the grassy compound and beat a hasty retreat.

The emperors who built Gondar were long dead, their grand castles now in ruins. I could not help but wonder what would be the fate of the current monarch and his capital built in a rush to bring the nation into the modern era. Rumors were circulating that a severe drought had begun the previous year in northern Wollo Province, causing a famine and resulting in thousands of deaths in the countryside. There were no reports either in local newspapers or radio broadcasts. Attempts by various organizations, concerned by stories of widespread starvation, to raise funds for famine relief were thwarted by a government too complacent to acknowledge the disaster.

Early the next day I set out as planned for my first trip to a Beta Israel village, Ambober, a small hamlet in the mountains about forty kilometers from Gondar. Since its founding during the Italian occupation in the late 1930s, the village had become the center of Beta Israel life in Begemder-Semien Province. Because of the village's proximity to Gondar and its accessibility to tourists, the people of Ambober were in frequent contact with the outside world. Yet despite a degree of modernization its prayer-house remained active. In a period when traditional Beta Israel religion was fast being replaced by new customs from abroad, an accessible village with four resident priests who still performed the traditional liturgy was a rich resource. It was in Ambober that I planned to do much of my research.

The local tourist association, capitalizing on the frequent arrival of prosperous American tourists interested in visiting the Falashas, charged nearly a hundred American dollars to rent a Land Rover and driver to transport them to Ambober. This sum was prohibitive for me, but it was possible to take a local bus or taxi to Tadda, a small town on the main road, and then travel by foot or on horseback over a rough track the remaining ten kilometers to the village. For a modest sum, young boys of the area would act as porters.

Several Beta Israel families lived in Tadda, one headed by Makonnen, a teacher who had learned Hebrew and who talked often of emigrating to Israel. Makonnen was a wiry, balding man with a crooked smile. His modest house was decorated inside with brightly colored posters of Israel and other mementos of Jewish life abroad brought to him by visitors. Makonnen spoke reasonably fluent English and was always ready to share a cup of tea and dreams of Jerusalem while he secured arrangements for the trip to Ambober.

That first day, while waiting for the men who were to accompany me to arrive, Makonnen and I went to the nearby *tedj bet*. It was early afternoon and an *azmari*, a musician who played the one-stringed lute, was performing before a small but jocular group of men. Makonnen and I sat down and ordered beers. The *azmari* was singing a spirited *shillela*, a song traditionally performed to rouse a warrior before battle. The *shillela* begins with a high, piercing cry, then descends to describe past glories or the exploits of a particular hero.

When the *azmari* began his next song, Makonnen and the others began to laugh. I struggled to understand the words. This was made more difficult because in Ethiopian poetry, whether in the Amharic vernacular or in classical Ethiopic (Ge'ez), each word or phrase may have a dual meaning. This verbal and literary device is called "wax and gold," referring to the "lost wax" process by which gold is cast. The goldsmith melts the wax positive within a clay mold, leaving a hollow space to be filled by the molten gold. Thus, the wax is the obvious, outer meaning, while the true, hidden significance of the text is the gold.

This musician was very clever indeed—he parodied a type of Ethiopian Christian hymn called a *melk'e*, traditionally sung in praise of a saint. Verses of the *melk'e* list parts of the saint's body that are preserved as relics. In this instance the *azmari* was singing about parts of my body, beginning with my hair and working his way downward. Uncertain whether to react with humor or embarrassment, I gulped my beer. As Makonnen and I left, the singer was praising the surmised virtues of my breasts.

The next surprise came as we arrived back at Makonnen's hut to join the Ambober residents who were to accompany me to the village. Two young boys had been recruited to carry my possessions. Since Ambober was about ten kilometers away and the track leading to it quite mountainous, Makonnen had suggested that I might want to rent a horse for the princely fee of two Ethiopian dollars. I had eagerly accepted. What I found waiting was a mangy horse, buzzing with flies, kicking irritably in the dirt. I decided to walk and one of the men mounted instead.

Our party included two teachers, the village "dresser" who had been trained in basic medical procedures by a visiting doctor several years before, and the two youngsters loaded down with my pack, tape recorder, and miscellaneous supplies. Forty-five minutes and a couple of kilometers up the path, the horse began to look more attractive. I mounted and the men immediately began laughing as I tried to arrange my long, denim skirt in a reasonably modest way. After inquiring if I had a pair of jeans with me, they suggested I change clothes. I was quite reluctant since I had been advised that a woman in jeans would offend local sensibilities, but I had brought a pair along to wear in my sleeping bag at night. With considerable misgivings, I ducked behind a tree and changed.

At a leisurely pace, the trip took about two and a half hours. The path led through cultivated fields covered by golden grain. The crops were guarded from marauding bands of baboons by young shepherds perched on makeshift platforms. One played his *washint*, a four-holed bamboo flute. The music would frighten away birds and other predators tempted by the ripening crops, as well as mask sudden noises that might cause a grazing flock of sheep or cattle to stampede. It also provided a pleasant diversion during the long, still hours the young boy was on watch.

The sound of the flute faded as the rough track wound up a high ridge of hills thickly covered with vegetation. As we passed a shady turn one teacher turned to me and said, "You have to be careful when you go through this place. There may be trouble here."

At the time I thought he was warning me against bandits, called *shifta*, said to roam the countryside and prey on the unwary. Only later, after repeated warnings in this and other overgrown spots, did I realize I was being cautioned not about thieves, but about a type of local spirit said to lurk in dark and sheltered areas, waiting for a chance to attack a passerby. Most Ethiopians believe in a number of spirits that have the capacity to affect a person's health and well-being. Individuals of all religious groups—Christian, Moslem, Falasha, and followers of other autochthonous traditions—also observe special rites of the *zar* cult to exorcise these spirits that can inhabit an individual and cause sickness or misfortune. Anyone with unusual characteristics—great beauty or good fortune, for example—is thought to be particularly vulnerable to the spirits' power. As a foreigner and a woman I was considered to be at risk.

Many nights in the villages I would hear the drumming at the *zar* rituals. I asked a few times if I might attend. "The children are just playing and dancing," the priests would tell me, and I was never allowed to observe. They were uncomfortable with my interest in these traditions at odds with both their traditional religion and the practices of Western Judaism that were slowly transforming their lives.

Though I soon stopped trying to attend these rituals I came later to understand them to some degree. One needed explanations for the many inexplicable tragedies—disease, hunger, violence—that were part of rural Ethiopian life. The elaborate rituals of the priests, chanted in a language only the clergy could understand, seemed to have little impact on daily village life outside the prayerhouse. In contrast, *zar* cult rituals addressed local and personal problems in a more immediate way, seeking to cure a particular patient or remedy a specific crisis.

The priests had little choice but to tolerate the *zar* rituals despite the multiple pressures they felt to halt these performances. In the past, the unordained musicians who had helped chant the Beta Israel liturgy, called *debtera* like their Christian counterparts, had been expert in writing amulets to protect individuals from a variety of malevolent spirits. By the 1970s, these *debtera* had largely disappeared from Beta Israel villages, along with their dual roles as musician in one tradition and magician in another.

As we arrived at the crest of the ridge, Gondar could be seen cradled in mountains to the northwest. Ambober was also visible, across a valley and beyond another ridge. But the distance fooled the eye, and we had to cross a stream and climb another steep hill before arriving at the village.

3

IN A BETA ISRAEL VILLAGE

Ambober was in many ways a microcosm of modern Beta Israel life. Flanked on three sides by mountains, the village was named "place of water" because of the presence of underground springs. The area had once been heavily forested, but construction as well as the selling of firewood had destroyed many of the trees.

Around four hundred Falashas lived in or immediately adjacent to the village. They planted crops such as barley, corn, chick peas, and *tef*, the grain used to make *injera*. Most derived at least part of their income from crafts. Some men were metalworkers who fashioned plows, knives, and other implements over an open fire, using animal-skin bellows to fan the flames. Others in the community worked as weavers, spinning the white cotton cloth used for clothing. Many of the women worked clay to make pottery they sold at local markets. Not only did these occupations barely provide a subsistence-level income, they entailed other liabilities.

Any Ethiopian who performs manual crafts, particularly a metalworker, is thought to be *buda,* a carrier of the evil eye. The people of Ambober, like other Ethiopians practicing crafts, were feared by many of their neighbors as *buda* people, and were said to be particularly dangerous at night when they were thought to have the power to become hyenas and prey upon others.

As we approached the village a number of children ran to greet us, and men and women looked up from their work to acknowledge our arrival with a bow of the head. The immediate friendliness and warmth of the Beta Israel community in Ambober dispelled any concern I might have had about my long-anticipated first visit to the village. After a discussion with the village elders it was decided that I would sleep in the schoolhouse, which had stone walls and a corrugated tin roof and was one of the more substantial structures in the village. To stay in someone's home was out of the question, since large families were already overflowing their round, single-room huts. Indeed, very often the home might shelter not only the family, but also a valued goat, chicken, donkey, or other livestock. I had originally hoped to locate an empty hut in which I might stay, and had even dreamed about duplicating the experience of a colleague who had once commissioned and then photographed the construction of her own house. But Ambober was crowded that fall, and no one expressed enthusiasm about building another house, even at my expense. So I settled for camping in the privacy and security of the superintendent's office at the village school.

Other than the evidence of the various crafts that typified Falasha life, Ambober was in many ways a typical Ethiopian village. Individual huts were surrounded by bushes and makeshift fences, each compound connected to others by rough paths. Ambober also had several mud-walled square or rectangular buildings with tin roofs, one housing a small clinic, others homes of teachers or additional buildings in the school compound. There was no power source in the village, but there was considerable evidence of aid from abroad, including the clinic with its basic stock of medical supplies, the large school compound, and a newly constructed well giving villagers access to an uncontaminated source of water.

At the center of the village stood the prayerhouse, a square building with stone walls and a metal roof, shaded by junipers and oleasters and surrounded by a rough fence. The whitewashed structure had two doors, one opening to the east, the other to the west. Inside, cloth was draped around the corners of the single large room, giving the feel of the circular shape once traditional for Beta Israel prayerhouses and still common to the architecture of most Ethiopian Christian churches.

The changing names of the prayerhouse illustrate the shifting Beta Israel world. Originally it had been called the *masgid*, the same name used for the mosque among Ethiopian Moslems. The term derives from a root meaning "to bow," and probably related originally to the Beta Israel (and Moslem) custom of bowing repeatedly upon entry to the prayerhouse and during certain prayers. But the building was also known as *selot bet*, literally "prayerhouse," the term that most Beta Israel priests used when I was in the village. Hebrew-speaking Falashas and those familiar with Jewish traditions abroad had begun, however, to refer to the prayerhouse by the Hebrew expression *bet knesset*. The building itself reflects these changes in name and orientation— on the roof is a recently mounted Star of David fashioned by a Beta Israel metalworker, and inside is found a new wooden Ark housing ritual items provided by Jews from abroad.

The Beta Israel prayerhouse can serve as a metaphor for the co-existence of old and new in Falasha religious life. It is an amalgam of old Beta Israel architecture and new Western Jewish symbols. The prayerhouse's function is equally syncretic—it is used for traditional Beta Israel rituals in the Ge'ez language as well as the newly introduced Hebrew liturgy.

This complicated juxtaposition of old and new in Falasha life is the result of over a century of change. The beginning of the transition can be dated to the mid-1860s, when the French scholar Joseph Halévy came to Ethiopia as an emissary of the Alliance Israélite Universelle, sent to investigate a people, said to have Jewish traditions, living in the northwest of the country. Halévy's mission was straightforward: he was to contact the Falashas and to purify their religious practices. After centuries of exclusion from the mainstream of Ethiopian society as an ethnic, occupational, and religious minority, the Falasha were to be told that their tradition as the House of Israel was shared with people from distant places. Halévy went about his work with zeal, setting into motion a process that would alter Beta Israel custom and belief.

Halévy's mission and the subsequent process of gaining recognition from Jewish circles abroad carried a price. From the first, Halévy freely criticized Beta Israel practices that were at odds with modern Judaism. Once, when presented with an amulet to protect him as he left a Beta Israel village, Halévy rejected the gift, lecturing its maker on his failure to believe only in the power of God. Those traditions that Halévy could not persuade the Beta Israel to change or modify, he tried to rationalize. He characterized the Beta Israel monks, who lived in monasteries on the outskirts of most villages and served as the religious leaders of their communities, as widowers who sought a life of contemplation. Later visitors were not so charitable and actively encouraged the Beta Israel to discontinue their monastic tradition.

For centuries the Beta Israel had clung to an identity that entailed considerable sacrifice. They had largely rejected the efforts of European Christian missionaries to convert them, and in general had shunned contact with outsiders. Why, then, did they respond so quickly and positively to Halévy's initiative? One can only speculate that Halévy, and all that he represented, elicited a deep emotional response.

Halévy's sympathetic approach was a watershed event, in part because the European Christian missionaries who had arrived in the area a decade or two earlier viewed the Beta Israel, and Christian Ethiopians as well, with thinly veiled contempt. Shortly before Halévy's arrival tensions had arisen between the Beta Israel and the missionaries, and the Ethiopian authorities themselves had had to become involved in resolving a series of disputes.

A scholar familiar with Ethiopian languages, Halévy was also a Jew who approached the Beta Israel as no one before him had been willing or able to do—as a coreligionist who shared a common framework of belief in one God. It seems likely that the emotional connection Halévy forged with the many Beta Israel villagers he encountered gave rise to the lasting impact of his brief stay.

Halévy's student Jacques Faitlovitch arrived in 1905 to continue his mentor's work. He was warmly welcomed by the Beta Israel, who had declined in number after a devastating wave of famine and disease that had swept the highlands in the late nineteenth century. Faitlovitch shared Halévy's commitment to "modernizing" Falasha Judaism and set into motion changes of which

Halévy could only have dreamed. Faitlovitch opened a school to train Beta Israel youngsters in modern Judaism, sent others to Europe and Palestine for higher education, and initiated an international campaign for Falasha recognition and support. Like Halévy, Faitlovitch saw his effort with the Falashas as a near-sacred mission, charged with the paradoxical aim of both rescuing these people and transforming their tradition.

Throughout the first half of the twentieth century pro-Falasha organizations around the world publicized the cause of the Ethiopian Jews. The founding of the state of Israel in 1948 provided a national and institutional focus for these activities and the growing Beta Israel identification with Jews abroad.

By the late 1950s, Western philanthropists had established Jewish schools in a number of Beta Israel villages in the Gondar region. Hebrew and Jewish liturgy were introduced and Western Jewish practices and identity became an integral part of Falasha daily life. Around 1950 the Falasha liturgical calendar was revised to incorporate post-biblical Jewish observances with which the people had previously been unfamiliar. Many traditional aspects of Beta Israel religious life were reshaped and renamed—and the *masgid* became the synagogue.

In light of the dramatic changes in Beta Israel life and belief that occurred during the century of transition beginning in the 1860s, the number of older customs and beliefs that survive is surprising. When I arrived in their villages in 1973, many of the Beta Israel—while actively seeking a new life and identity abroad—still maintained many aspects of a powerful tradition centuries old.

The dynamics of change and the many conflicts that were their legacy were not far beneath the surface in a village like Ambober. But a number of factors masked the extraordinarily complicated situation from most visitors.

The outsider's point of view was shaped by a literature pervaded by sectarian bias. The early competition between Western Christians and Jews over Falasha religious allegiance and belief had been largely replaced in the twentieth century by a growing debate over Falasha origins and religious identity. By mid-century a campaign had been launched to insure formal recognition of the group as Jews by religious authorities in Israel. To buttress the case for recognition, supporters romanticized and mythologized the Beta Israel past, proposing connections with diverse peoples and places in Jewish antiquity. Even among scholars speculation based on tenuous evidence replaced even-handed inquiry. The Beta Israel were variously proposed to be converts of Jewish immigrants from southern Arabia or Egypt, or descendants of Jews who accidentally traveled south either at the time of the Exodus from Egypt or after the destruction of the Second Temple in Jerusalem. Beta Israel origins were considered to be separate from those of other Ethiopians, despite the fact that the Ethiopian Christian majority also traced its descent to King Solomon.

By the early 1970s the Beta Israel community, numbering perhaps twenty-five thousand, had moved into an unequivocal alignment with the outside Jewish world. The Beta Israel had always shared belief and worldview with Jews. After a century of increasing contact they shared many more aspects of Jewish ritual and custom.

My own recognition of the tension in Beta Israel life and identity developed slowly since my perspective, too, had been shaped by the existing literature. With virtually everything I read suggesting that Falasha tradition preserved elements of ancient Jewish practice, I had spent over a year studying Ethiopian languages and Jewish liturgy in Jerusalem before coming to Ethiopia. In Jerusalem I became familiar with the controversy over Beta Israel origins and religious identity, and its ongoing political ramifications.

I also met members of the Ethiopian community in Israel and arrived in Ambober with tape-recorded messages from these friends and relatives now living abroad. The many hours spent in different homes, playing and replaying these tapes, solidified the warm welcome I had at first received. The Ambober teachers, two of whom had studied in Israel as teenagers and spoke Hebrew, went out of their way to ease my adjustment.

Many villagers would help me practice useful phrases in Amharic, laughing at my awkward accent and frequent errors. I became the object of much good-natured joking. When I was alone in the schoolhouse children would stop by to visit and talk, often sharing a few kernels of roasted corn. One teenager played a *masenqo* with a hand-carved, wooden Star of David mounted on top. He performed an eclectic repertory, alternating Hebrew holiday songs such as "Who Knows One?" with popular Ethiopian melodies. Once he serenaded me with an improvised number entitled "Kay Kaufman *malkam wazero nat.*" The translation—"Kay Kaufman is a nice lady"!

My first trip to Ambober fell just before the eve of the New Year, a holiday traditionally called *Berhan Saraqa*, literally "The Light Appeared," or *Tazkara Abraham*, "Commemoration of Abraham." Although most villagers now referred to the holiday by the Hebrew name *Rosh Hashanah*, they still celebrated a very traditional *Berhan Saraqa*, attending the rituals performed by their religious leaders, the *qes*, or priests.

The sun had just set behind the mountains when prayers began for *Berhan Saraqa* eve. I sat on a chair in the center of the prayerhouse with my tape recorder on my lap. The wooden table opposite me held a smoky oil lamp that cast a weak glow, barely enough to light a silkscreen of Jerusalem tacked on the whitewashed wall opposite. In contrast to the eternal flame common to universal Jewish tradition, the lamp was rekindled anew before each ritual began. Five priests, dressed in white gowns and turbans, swayed and chanted a prayer service in Ge'ez. One rang out a repetitive rhythm on a flat, circular metal gong, while a second struck a large kettledrum covered with the same bright, flowered cloth I had seen in Ethiopian Christian churches.

About fifty people crowded into the small room, mainly residents of Ambober and nearby hamlets. The men, each draped in a white *shamma*, stood to my right, attentive to the priests but unable to participate because they did not know Ge'ez. Women sat on the grass-covered dirt floor around the perimeter, listening silently, while children huddled nearby, whispering, giggling, and only occasionally watching the proceedings with big, dark eyes. After half an hour of singing, the priests ended the ritual by blessing the congregation. They then turned to me and acknowledged my presence with handshakes. "*Shabbat shalom,*" they greeted me in Hebrew, and I answered, "*Shabbat shalom*" (Sabbath peace). Then they asked me to play back the tape I had just recorded.

The Ge'ez ritual for *Berhan Saraqa* eve and morning was unlike anything I had seen or studied in Jewish liturgical tradition. The priests divided themselves into two choruses, or, as they termed it, "two sides." One side repeated the verse initiated by the other, singing the same melody over and over for as much as an hour at a time. The regular rhythm of the drum and gong and the steady alternation between sides was hypnotic.

Many of the prayers for the *Berhan Saraqa* holiday contained praise of Egzi'abher, the name for God in Ge'ez. These prayers contained texts of praise and supplication to a God who is the "crown of the poor" and the "strength of the weak." Scattered through the same rituals were also texts in a special Falasha dialect similar to those spoken by other Agau peoples known to have been among Ethiopia's earliest inhabitants. With the exception of a few words, the Agau passages were not understood by priest or layman.

The only part of the Beta Israel New Year celebration familiar to me was a Hebrew prayer service led on New Year's morning by a group of young Falashas who had refused to attend the Ge'ez ritual. They used familiar melodies learned during studies in Israel and from Western Jewish visitors. During the Hebrew services the wooden cabinet in the eastern corner of the room was opened, exposing a miniature Torah scroll, Jewish prayer shawls, and Hebrew prayerbooks donated by Jews from abroad. The Hebrew service was held facing this makeshift Ark, but on all other occasions the cabinet remained unopened and the priests prayed in the opposite corner of the room.

I was surprised but relieved that the Beta Israel priests permitted me to record in the prayerhouse on holidays and the Sabbath. Mechanical devices are prohibited in Orthodox Jewish synagogues and I knew that the Beta Israel had always kept the Sabbath and holidays rigorously. The priests explained, however, that since my tape recorder did not require the lighting of fire it did not violate their religious laws. Thus I was able to record rituals in the prayerhouse on all occasions. This was a great boon since prayer services could never be recreated in full, and the priests found it difficult to sing prayers separately since each one was linked to the next in a manner that helped them remember the order of service.

Though the Ambober priests would perform the Ge'ez liturgy in the prayerhouse on holidays and Sabbaths when they were in the village, on many occasions one or all were absent, attending to people in villages without priests or performing other duties. At these times the prayerhouse remained closed. When the priests were at home, they observed most holidays on the eve with a short ritual around sundown. Morning holiday services began between 3:00 and 4:00 A.M. and lasted several hours. Daily morning and evening prayer services were almost never performed since practical responsibilities took precedence. During the fall of 1973 I managed to record only one daily morning ritual, performed by one accommodating priest to satisfy my repeated requests.

On some occasions there were all-night vigils in the prayerhouse, such as on the Sabbath of Sabbaths, a unique celebration held every seven weeks. Priests from surrounding Beta Israel villages would come to Ambober to join the resident priests on this occasion. Once I witnessed a Sabbath of Sabbaths ritual mounted by ten priests.

After the brief Friday evening ritual at sunset, the priests spent the evening at individual homes, drinking tea and listening to transistor radios carrying reports of growing tensions in the Middle East. At around 10:00 P.M. they returned to the prayerhouse and resumed prayers. They then chanted throughout the night, the austerity of the ritual enhanced by the absence on the Sabbath of the drum and gong otherwise used to accompany the services.

Around 2:00 A.M. there was a sudden pause in the singing, and the cold, dark prayerhouse fell silent. The head priest uncovered a large clay pot sitting in the corner and turned to me. He asked in Amharic, "Would you like to drink *tella* with us?" *Tella* is a beer made from fermented barley. For an hour we sat in the prayerhouse and drank, everyone becoming increasingly convivial, even rowdy. Revived, the priests again began praying, until around 9:00 A.M. when, exhausted, everyone dispersed to village homes to get some rest.

But the Sabbath of Sabbaths observance was still not complete. At noon the priests again congregated in the prayerhouse. They sang until around 4:00 P.M., when another *tella* break was announced. This time everyone went to the home of Priest Ya'qob, at around the age of fifty, one of the younger village priests. I joined the men, drinking alongside them while Priest Ya'qob's wife remained quietly in the background, approaching only to refill our glasses.

Late in the afternoon Priest Ya'qob accompanied me to the school so that I could rest before the evening ritual concluding the Sabbath day. He promised to come back and collect me before evening prayers began, since during unescorted walks through the village I was inevitably bothered by the vicious dogs that roamed the area. But around sunset I heard singing in the distance and realized that the service had begun without me. Throwing caution aside I grabbed my tape recorder and dashed from the school compound to the prayerhouse. The priests, continuing to drink *tella* long after my departure, had forgotten all about me.

I found them dancing in a large circle, jumping up and down with a shake of the body reminiscent of a popular Ethiopian shoulder dance called *iskista*. They accompanied these movements with loud, raspy breathing and the pounding of their wooden prayer staffs upon the ground. After several minutes they stopped dancing and concluded the prayers, acknowledging me only to ask that I play back portions of the day's ritual for all to hear.

Afterward, I was invited to one of the teachers' homes to drink coffee and to eat the special leavened bread which on the Sabbath replaces the flat *injera*. As we sat drinking and talking in the small house, billows of smoke suddenly blew in through the open doorway. My host, Dan'el, jumped up, dashed outside, and shouted for help. A fire had started in the adjoining thatched-roof hut that he had constructed to shelter his wife and newborn son during the forty days of isolation mandated for women after childbirth. People hurriedly grabbed whatever water they had in clay vessels in their homes and came to douse the flames, while others ran to the well to gather more. Dan'el succeeded in rescuing his terrified wife and baby, but the isolation hut was completely destroyed. After several tense minutes, the fire was contained.

I tried to comfort Dan'el's shaken wife and screaming infant son, thankful that they had not been injured. I also realized that this was the first time that I had seen her other than at a distance. Although I was a woman alone in rural Ethiopia my relationship with Beta Israel women was quite formal. The distance between us was a result of our vastly different roles and status. Although Ethiopian women keep their own names after marriage and have certain traditional legal rights, they are expected to remain very much in the background within the home. An Ethiopian woman, even in the urban areas, might not be presented to guests, and she certainly would not eat until the men and other visitors had completed their meals.

Before I arrived in Ethiopia, a female anthropologist who had once lived for some months in Falasha villages sounded a warning: if I wished to interact closely with Beta Israel men, particularly the clergy, I must be careful to maintain my distance from the women of the community. Otherwise I would jeopardize my status and severely limit my access to the males with whom I must work.

From the beginning I had been treated like a marginal male. In turn, I began to wear jeans regularly, as I had been requested to do during my first horseback ride out to the village, and put away the modest denim skirts I had brought along. Always I was included at drinking parties and served food with the men. It soon became clear that as long as I carried my tape recorder and other scholarly paraphernalia my access to the men was assured. This was confirmed on several occasions when I was urged to bring the taping equipment along despite the absence of a musical event to record. The portable reel-to-reel Uher field recorder somehow became my male apparatus.

Yet while the men cooperated fully with my research and included me in social activities related to the liturgical cycle, I was never really a part of their world. Though without exception they were kind to me and solicitous of my welfare, there was rarely a spontaneous, personal exchange. Our conversations were limited for the most part to discussions of Beta Israel tradition and the religious life that I had come to study. It seemed to me that when I was present social gatherings were subdued, and I often felt that the men were constrained by my presence. The most spontaneous and lively conversations were inevitably about the situation of the Falasha community in Israel and their own prospects for emigration. While there is no doubt that my distinctive status enabled me to accomplish efficiently most of my research goals, it established an almost insurmountable barrier to establishing really meaningful personal relationships in the village context.

With only one woman did I achieve what charitably could be termed a friendship. Alganesh, the wife of Priest Mika'el, was a woman in her late thirties who had given birth to ten children. During one of my early visits to the village her husband brought me to their home for coffee. When he was called away for a brief priestly duty shortly after we arrived, Alganesh and I found ourselves alone, or at least the only two adults in the midst of numerous small children, several chickens, and a friendly goat.

We sat down by the fire burning in the open hearth in the center of the hut. Smoke filtered up and out tiny openings in the conical roof. The children jostled around, a few playing with small stones on and under the rickety sleeping platforms that jutted out from the walls. Alganesh washed raw coffee beans, browned them, ground them with a stone, and brewed strong, bitter Ethiopian coffee in a black clay pot. She was a slight woman with closely cropped hair, wearing a stained dress of heavy Ethiopian cotton.

We spoke at length about her eldest son, who, with support from individuals abroad, had studied in Jewish schools in Europe.

He later emigrated to Israel, where I had met him in Jerusalem before my own departure for Ethiopia. On my first day in Ambober I had given Priest Mika'el a snapshot I had taken of their son only a few months before. At Alganesh's urging I reviewed the details of his new life. Alganesh spoke movingly of her longing to see her son and to join him in Israel. Next, she began asking me questions. Why did I choose to stay so far away from my family? Why did I not have a husband and children?

"I wanted to come to Ethiopia, to live here with you, and to learn about your music," I said. "Later I can have a family, too, if I wish."

Alganesh shook her head slowly, and answered in a soft voice. "Maybe you are lucky. You will not have too many children. I am frightened about what will happen to me."

She spoke of her concern about complications suffered during the birth of her last child and her inadequate milk supply afterward. Frightened of yet another but seemingly inevitable pregnancy, she asked if I could help. I promised to speak to people at the hospital in Gondar, and later found out that both birth-control measures and sterilization were readily available. But Alganesh never did visit the Gondar clinic for the appointment I arranged, despite my offer to pay the expenses. She only murmured, the next time we met, that her husband simply would not allow her to go.

Though Priest Mika'el and I never discussed the matter, I have little doubt that I overstepped the bounds of propriety in that instance, however good my intentions. The future of my relationship with Alganesh was also made clear a couple of weeks later, when I arrived one day in the village after a brief break in Gondar. Priest Mika'el invited me to his home and I readily accepted, glad of an opportunity to see Alganesh as well. As we entered their compound I was surprised to see her sitting in the doorway of a thatched hut some meters apart from the main house, obviously in isolation during menstruation. Traditionally, a Beta Israel woman is forbidden to touch anyone during menstruation or after childbirth—someone else prepares her food and leaves it outside the isolation hut for her use. Yet despite the traditional prohibition two women from the village sat nearby talking with Alganesh, and her children also gathered around her, jumping on and off her lap.

I did not know how to react. To touch a woman during menstruation was to violate an old taboo, but not to greet a friend properly was also offensive. I decided to chance a greeting and started to approach the hut, but Priest Mika'el took my arm and said sharply, "Come with me into the house."

At the time, I interpreted this experience as reaffirming my unique status, one shared only with other foreign women who pursued research in outlying areas. A monk who encountered my colleague Marilyn in northern Ethiopia commented: "While our mothers are in the kitchen, you wander the world." I, too, had left the kitchen and, empowered by the vagaries of nationality, gender, and economic privilege, had chosen to explore other worlds. But I would learn that in gaining access to even limited aspects of the male experience I had immeasurably complicated the possibility of meaningful personal relationships with either women or men.

During those first weeks in the north I witnessed the celebration of the major annual holidays shared by the Beta Israel with other Jews. After *Berhan Saraqa*, the New Year celebration, came *Astasreyo*, comparable to the Jewish Day of Atonement. For *Astasreyo*, which by 1973 most Ambober Falashas had come to call by the Hebrew name *Yom Kippur*, the priests once again celebrated a vigil beginning on the eve and continuing throughout the day of the observance.

For a Western Jew accustomed to sober observance on the day of repentance, the Beta Israel *Astasreyo* was an extraordinary contrast. The Ethiopian fast did not start until well after sundown, as the villagers, including the priests, ate a leisurely dinner to prepare themselves for the long night to come. Around 9:00 P.M. Priest Mika'el entered the prayerhouse and lit a single candle. The teacher Dan'el then kindled two small candles in memory of his deceased parents, a practice he had adopted as a student during the 1950s in Israel.

The ritual began around 9:30 P.M. in a partially filled prayerhouse. As each man and woman entered, they bowed low. The women sometimes touched their foreheads to stones on the ground, a penitential act. During prayers, members of the congregation would occasionally bow repeatedly, touching their foreheads to the grass-covered dirt floor. At the beginnings of important prayers, and at mention of the name of Egzi'abher, God, the women would raise their voices in high-pitched cries of ululation.

The tone of the service was almost joyful and the undercurrent of noise from the congregation continued unabated until many dropped off to sleep. In their white turbans and garments, leaning upon the wooden prayer staffs, the priests swayed like ghosts in the faint light. From time to time they conserved their strength by taking turns singing, each one resting for a time upon the long wooden bench that stretched along the west wall of the room.

The night passed slowly as I tediously changed tapes, trying not to miss any of the ritual. The priests, now accustomed to my presence, paused as I ministered to the tape recorder and began again only after a new tape was wound and running. By the early morning hours only the subdued singing of one or two priests at a time could be heard, as their colleagues and the congregation slept. Finally there was silence for an hour, with only night sounds and an occasional snore breaking the quiet. I buttoned my sweater to keep out the chill and rested my head upon the tape recorder, grateful for a short respite.

Before dawn the service resumed, and by first light the packed prayerhouse began to stir. The chatter of children and cries of babies bundled on their mothers' backs provided a counterpoint to the repetitive melodies. Birds chirped and clattered about on the metal roof. A few individuals came forward and placed before the priests small sums of money or bundles of wound thread. I momentarily wondered if I should make a contribution, but decided against it since I was unsure exactly what the custom meant.

I was relieved that I hadn't acted impulsively when I later learned that these were penitential offerings, demonstrating a sincere repentance for sins.

For two hours during the morning the priests deferred to the young Beta Israel men, who performed portions of the Western Jewish liturgy in Hebrew. The priests stood aside, their faces almost hidden by the large Jewish prayer shawls they draped over their turbans. After the Hebrew morning liturgy was completed, the priests put away the prayer shawls, assumed their usual positions, and continued the vigil.

In the middle of the afternoon the singing stopped and the priests called for silence. For the first time during my stay, they brought forth the Ge'ez Bible, the *Orit*, and placed it on the small table near the oil lamp. Priest Mika'el carefully removed the protective cover of flowered cloth and opened the large manuscript. Alongside the *Orit*, the head priest, Alaqa Gete, laid a miniature Hebrew *Torah* scroll presented to the village a few months earlier by a Jewish visitor.

The priests debated where to begin. Eventually they agreed, and Priest Mika'el began reading aloud in Ge'ez, with his cousin, Priest Ruben, translating into the vernacular. After completing the Ten Commandments and other portions from the Book of Exodus, Priest Mika'el gently rewrapped the *Orit*. Next he uncovered the small Hebrew *Torah* scroll, holding it aloft for all to see. The women ululated exultantly. Finally, both holy books were wrapped in cloth and put away in the wooden cabinet, side by side on a single shelf.

Late in the afternoon the priests suddenly rose and began to dance, moving in a circle, their prayer staffs bobbing up and down. Priest Ruben turned to me and said, "You'd better take your tape recorder outside. There will be a lot of dust."

Soon, the entire congregation was on its feet and began to jump up and down. Even two stern-looking armed men who had stood threateningly in one corner since early morning participated, leaning their rifles against the wall. As everyone began to cough from the choking dust that was raised, the priests called for order and the jumping stopped. According to the priests the tradition stems from a Beta Israel belief that one must fast and exercise on *Astasreyo* until exhausted.

The ritual ended shortly after sunset, but not before the teachers again interpolated a brief late afternoon service in Hebrew. As night fell everyone retired to village homes to break the fast and rest from the lengthy ritual.

I returned to Dan'el's house, where we turned on a shortwave transistor radio to hear the news. We ate *injera* and roasted corn and drank coffee, listening in shock and silence to reports of the first tragic day of the Yom Kippur War between Egypt and Israel. Unaware of the events so many miles away, young children continued dancing and singing Ethiopian songs in celebration of the conclusion of the fast.

The following morning saw a juxtaposition of the tragic and ludic. Many adults had disregarded their usual routines to gather around village radios, particularly the one shortwave set that could pick up international broadcasts from the BBC. Everyone was further sobered by news that a child in a nearby village had died, and that the priests needed to perform a funeral.

The teachers, trying to distract the children confused by the black mood, went to the school office and opened parcels that had arrived before the holiday from an American clothing manufacturer. Hearing of the shortage of clothing in Beta Israel villages, this well-meaning patron had sent a variety of red-and-yellow calico peasant blouses and skirts. The children rushed into the school, grabbing any article of clothing within reach. Young Beta Israel boys, dressed in brightly colored blouses and skirts, wandered around the schoolyard, looking for all the world as if they were ready to attend a square dance.

I passed the morning trying to be helpful, penning a tactful thank-you note to the donor for a well-intentioned but inappropriate gift. My own mood was low. I was exhausted from the ritual of the previous day and upset by the news from Israel. As I looked around at the children, flies crawling in their eyes, I reached a breaking point. I suddenly decided to leave for Gondar.

Only two small boys were available to accompany me, but I was determined to go despite storm clouds gathering over the mountains. We quickly prepared the horse and left the village, the kids singing lively Israeli songs to lift our mood and pace. As we neared Tadda, the skies opened up and a torrential rainstorm began. I clutched the tape recorder under my raincoat, holding tight the reins with the other hand. Just as we arrived on the outskirts of the village, the saddle suddenly gave way and slipped off, carrying me with it to the ground. Landing on my side, I somehow shielded both the tape recorder and myself from the fall. After delivering the horse to a startled Makonnen, we managed to flag down a bus on the main road. I arrived home in Gondar several hours later, wet, dirty, and exhausted.

When I returned to Ambober a few days later, everyone was preoccupied with news of the struggle in the Middle East. At the opening rituals for *Ba'ala Masallat*, the Beta Israel equivalent to the Jewish Festival of Booths (*Sukkot*), prayers were offered for the safety of Israel. For the remainder of the holiday season the mood was gloomy. Many in the village were frightened for their own welfare as well when unfounded rumors circulated that area Moslems planned to attack Beta Israel villages in a local version of the Yom Kippur hostilities.

There were additional blows to the Falasha community during the following days. Radio reports and the few newspapers that filtered north brought word that Ethiopia had broken longstanding and close relations with Israel. The hundreds of Israelis in Ethiopia, many involved in development work, would soon be leaving. The Israeli Embassy in Addis Ababa would also close within the week and El Al would suspend its regular Tel Aviv–Addis Ababa run. To many among the Beta Israel community, especially those spearheading the now-successful effort for recognition by Israel, their efforts to emigrate appeared doomed. The news was devastating.

Village life went on as in slow motion and even the ritual cycle was temporarily disrupted as Ambober priests went to outlying villages to offer comfort and blessings to others in the community.

The Beta Israel community was struggling to regain its equilibrium.

With the priests away I was quite isolated in the village. I also felt physically depleted, my back still aching from the bad fall. Perhaps sympathetically, my tape recorder had developed a background hum of unknown origin. I decided to return to Addis Ababa for a short visit to have my tape recorder repaired. But in my heart I knew that there were other reasons why I wanted to make that trip.

4

LIFE ON BENIN SEFER

A taxi delivered me to the grass field south of Gondar that
served as the airport. While the vintage DC-3 readied for
takeoff, someone ran out on the field to chase away several stray
cows grazing on the runway. As we gained altitude the plane
skipped between mountaintops nearly as high as the flight path.
I tried to relax despite the turbulence, understanding then why
the flights linking Ethiopia's famed historical sights were often
referred to as the "hysterical" tour. I sat back and began to anticipate my return to Addis Ababa, replaying in my mind what had
happened during my first, extraordinary stay in the capital.

Shortly after I had first arrived in Addis Ababa the previous
August, after I had established my daily routine of Amharic lessons and fieldwork preparation, I had begun to make my way
through a list of miscellaneous contacts in the Ethiopian capital. A variety of people had provided names of individuals who
might help fill any lonely hours. I delivered messages to families
of Ethiopian friends living in the United States and met a kindly
Eritrean priest, Father Marqos, who had once lived in Jerusalem.
Father Marqos became a trusted friend who regarded my safety as
his personal responsibility. An imposing figure in his black clerical
robe, he often accompanied me around the capital.

Friends in the U.S. State Department had also given me the
name of an official with one of the American relief organizations,
whom I contacted shortly after my arrival. Richard and his wife,
Susan, immediately invited me to their stone villa on the outskirts
of the capital and provided a good measure of advice about life
in urban Ethiopia.

Ten days later, in an attempt to reciprocate their warm hospitality, I invited Richard and Susan to lunch at the Villa Verde, a small, somewhat tattered Italian restaurant almost hidden in a stand of bougainvillea off one of the city's main thoroughfares. This and the many other Italian restaurants testified to the past occupation's lingering effect on Addis Ababa life.

After finishing a less than memorable but blessedly innocuous lasagna, I pulled out my address book to retrieve a name that I had not yet followed up.

"Do you know a family named Schelemay?" I asked, spelling the name since I was uncertain how to pronounce it.

"It's spelled without the *c*," Richard replied, "and is pronounced Shéll-a-may. Of course, everyone does."

"I was told they are something like the Jewish first family of Ethiopia," I ventured.

"That's correct. But unless you've got an 'in,' the permanent Jewish community in Addis Ababa keeps pretty much to itself. In fact, I've not met the Shelemays," Richard explained. "But everyone knows where their compound and offices are located, in the middle of the city. We can take you there after lunch."

Only shortly before my departure from Jerusalem to Addis Ababa had I learned of the presence of a permanent Jewish community numbering less than a hundred in Addis Ababa. It was composed of Jews who had lived for centuries in Aden, a port at the tip of southern Arabia that had become an outpost of the British Empire. The Adenite Jews were of Sephardic descent blended over the years through marriage with Jews from India, North Africa, Palestine, and Yemen who also found their way to the thriving port. In Addis Ababa most Adenite Jews were involved in foreign trade, and many owned shops selling imported clothing, materials, and other luxury items from Europe, the Near East, and Asia.

The Shelemay family was the largest of the Adenite clans, with all five sons and one of five daughters remaining in Ethiopia. The family lived and worked in a compound dominating an entire city block located on Benin Sefer (Benin Street) just below the piazza, the central shopping area of the capital. The family had built two multistory apartment buildings that hugged the steep hill, facing each other across the narrow two-lane road. One was a three-story white building, the other a taller, more modern structure with exposed concrete beams and red railings on the terraces. Beside the white building was a large asphalt-covered parking lot, flanked along its length by a corrugated steel warehouse, and surveyed on its uphill end by the Addis Ababa synagogue, perched atop a steep stone stairway. Along the street front on the ground floor of both buildings stretched shops and businesses, including an Ethiopian insurance company, an Italian hairdresser, a Chinese dentist, and for fully half the hundred-yard length of the white building, the Shelemay offices.

At the front door of this office, unmarked except for the presence of a white-haired guard in jodhpurs and *shamma*, I got out of the car.

"I'd like to see Mr. Shelemay," I said politely in Amharic.

"Which one?" asked the guard, waiting for my answer.

With no response forthcoming, he led me into the office, through a sparsely furnished reception area, and into a large, cluttered room with a desk near a window on the left and red leather sofas and chairs on the right. On the tables and in the corners of the room were piled stacks of brightly patterned textile samples. The guard gestured upward, and I looked up to see a loft housing yet another office. As I climbed the circular metal staircase a tall, dark-haired man in a pin-striped suit came into view, standing at the top.

"Jack Shelemay," he said, extending his hand and then directing me to a seat in an armchair in front of the cluttered desk. I introduced myself and sat down, self-consciously smoothing my crumpled clothing. I explained that I was a visiting scholar and that his family's name had been given to me by a well-known rabbi in Jerusalem who had visited them some years before.

"I don't remember meeting him," Jack Shelemay commented evenly. "Maybe he came when I was abroad."

With my contact unknown, and no other earthly reason for my visit, we made a few minutes of awkward conversation. Not knowing what else to say to this elegant man whose accent was located somewhere between the Middle East and England, I rose to leave.

"Maybe I'll see you on Saturday morning," I volunteered. "I plan to come to the synagogue to hear the service."

"If you do, stop by the office and say hello," he responded. "And in the meantime, good luck in the Peace Corps."

I fumed all the way down the stairs and out the door. I had fantasized about an invitation to a family gathering, hoping that the hospitality so abundant in other quarters would be forthcoming here as well. But now I was unsure if I were more aggravated not even to have been offered the customary cup of coffee or that my independent research had been mistaken for a Peace Corps project. This soft-spoken man with dark eyes had certainly written me off quickly, I thought.

The following Saturday morning I arrived as planned at the synagogue on the Shelemay compound. The synagogue was unlike any I had seen before—a small white structure built atop an arch beyond which lay an overgrown courtyard. Within the single room, benches were arranged along the walls according to Sephardic custom, with a podium and a velvet-curtained Ark holding the sacred scrolls in the center. Hebrew prayer books and prayer shawls spilled out of small niches along the walls, spaces once used, I was later told, by a former owner for storage of sacks of Maria-Theresa thalers.

I sat in a tiny alcove for women, little more than a closet with a lattice covering the opening to the main room. The service began, an eclectic mixture of Adenite, Yemenite, and other Sephardic liturgical traditions. At first I listened with interest, since a study of the music and ritual of the Adenite tradition appeared to be a possible fallback dissertation topic should my Falasha research not prove viable. But my mind wandered. I did not see Jack Shelemay among the dozen or so men praying in the adjoining room.

After an hour alone in the cramped, stuffy space, I went outside to get some air. I wandered downstairs, out through the compound, and turned left in front of the Shelemay offices, which appeared to be closed with their blinds drawn. I walked up and down several times, undecided if even to try the door which I now realized with disappointment must certainly be locked on the Sabbath. But I couldn't resist trying the handle, and as I grasped it, it opened. I stepped inside, and there sat Jack Shelemay at a desk just beyond the entry.

We both laughed, and the awkwardness of the first meeting quickly dissipated. "I wanted to get in touch with you, but didn't know where you were staying," Jack said. "If you had not come by today, I would have tried to locate you through the American Embassy on Monday. Would you like to have dinner tonight?"

Astonished, I smiled and accepted his invitation.

That first dinner was at an elegant restaurant run by a Swiss chef who had built a large following in the capital. Escargot, steak, fine wines, all were welcome diversions for Ethiopians and foreigners with the resources for a fashionable evening out. After dinner followed dancing and dessert at the Addis Ababa Hilton. The hotel was set in spacious, beautifully landscaped grounds near the emperor's palace. The building was of rough-cut stone, decorated with motifs of Ethiopian crosses in imitation of the famous tenth-century rock-hewn churches of Lalibela in the north of the country. To complete this theme the hotel overlooked a magnificent swimming pool built in the shape of an Ethiopian cross, filled with waters from the hot mineral springs running beneath.

At the hotel, worlds collided. *Injera* and *wat*, ordinarily eaten with the fingers, were served with knife, fork, and linen napkins in a formal dining room. Dance music reflected twentieth-century Africa facing West: four young Ethiopian musicians played arrangements of Ethiopian folk songs on saxophone, keyboard, vibes, and percussion. Their signature tune was the traditional Ethiopian melody *tezzeta*, "remembrance," a song of longing for lover or country, depending upon one's mood or situation.

We finished the evening around midnight at a ramshackle drive-in cafe that served flaming punch, a concoction of rum and other unidentifiable ingredients ignited before being served. I'd been introduced to an Ethiopia this scholar never knew existed.

The next day Jack called and proposed a drive south of Addis Ababa to Koka Dam, which housed a hydroelectric power station built after the war with reparations from Italy. Nearby was a luxurious vacation palace of Italian marble originally intended for the emperor's occasional use but later opened for public enjoyment. For years the emperor had returned occasionally to Koka Dam for lunch, greeting visitors at the now public restaurant as if they were his private guests and leading startled children by the hand through the gardens in back.

Our trip was less eventful since by mid-1973 the emperor no longer traveled the distance south over blacktop and gravel roads. He was growing old, though he made no sign of any intent to relinquish his power. We had lunch, admired the exotic flowers, and stood upon the dam with its view of the highland mountains meeting the flatter terrain to the south.

A full week of elegant dinners followed, a whirlwind tour of the cosmopolitan best that Addis Ababa had to offer. I was delighted with the experience, surprised and amused that such an active social life had materialized when I least expected it. I had come to Ethiopia prepared only for fieldwork. After a year and a half in Jerusalem I was tired of the effort and strain of cross-cultural dating and had looked forward to time on my own before returning home to the United States. So focused was I on my research that I had packed only two dresses, conservative, tailored shirtwaists in navy blue. I was all business, and this sudden rush of attention caught me off balance.

At first I simply decided to have a good time, to experience the type of fling one reads about in novels and is sure does not really exist. Certainly I was lonely and Jack promised to be a novel diversion. But as I talked to him for hours each evening, I discovered a remarkably kind and sophisticated man unlike anyone I'd ever known. Jack was a businessman immersed in international trade but also an avid reader, skilled photographer, and amateur anthropologist. Strong interests in theater and music had been honed during a decade in England, first at a Jewish boys' school in Brighton and later, while studying economics and literature in

London. Despite the differences in our backgrounds and lives I felt a rapport with this man. I was amazed by his sensitivity and amused by his sense of humor. The following Friday evening I received my first invitation to the Shelemay compound. The family occupied apartments in the building opposite the offices, the entrance watched by a bearded guard wrapped in a *shamma*. Designed by an Israeli architect once married to one of the Shelemay daughters, the building was a maze of different levels connected by short staircases, designed to accommodate the steep incline of Benin Sefer. The rear wall of the building was of louvered glass through which one could look down upon a sea of corrugated metal roofs and eucalyptus trees, and through which wafted the rhythmic work songs of women sorting coffee beans at a nearby warehouse. All the apartments stretched along the front of the building, most of them duplexes or triplexes with terraces on each level overlooking the street.

That night I met others in the Shelemay family for the first time. Jack and I were invited to his eldest brother's apartment, where the family usually congregated on the Sabbath, holidays, and many other quiet evenings. Salamone was a man in his fifties who had assumed the role of family patriarch since the death of his father during the previous year. A large man with an incipient potbelly, Salamone was a gregarious host whose speech and mannerisms somehow reminded me of Anwar Sadat. He and his wife, Alicia, greeted me cordially and introduced another brother, Danny, and a sister, Aviva.

The Shelemay Sabbath dinner surpassed any fantasies I could have had concerning life in the compound on Benin Sefer. The dinner table sparkled with porcelain and silver. The conversation might have graced the Tower of Babel, moving with ease between Hebrew, English, and Italian, sprinkled with occasional Arabic tales and Amharic proverbs. I was surprised when I read the engraving on the traditional cup holding the Sabbath evening ritual wine—it was a wedding gift to Salamone and Alicia from Jacques Faitlovitch, the activist who had transformed Falasha traditions. Meanwhile young Ethiopian women, dressed somewhat incongruously in frilly white aprons and caps, served the meal. The main course was *fasolia*, a traditional Adenite concoction of meat and beans in a heavy tomato-based sauce. The chef was Salamone, who derived great pleasure from running the kitchen despite the bewildered presence of a full-time Ethiopian cook.

After dinner we adjourned to the living room for coffee and liqueur—and more conversation. I struggled to keep my head clear and to make a good impression. I was the object of great interest since Jack, a self-described confirmed bachelor, did not often invite female friends to the family table. I soon realized that Jack's dinner invitation had not been tendered lightly. By the time I left Addis Ababa a few weeks later for my first trip north to Gondar, we had already become involved in an intense relationship.

Jack and I had been in close touch by mail and telephone while I was in Gondar and the villages, and when my flight arrived in Addis Ababa, he was waiting at the airport to pick me up in his shiny green Rover. We drove into town, heading up Churchill Road to Faye's house at Tewodros Square. Jack drove around the circle, but instead of turning into the driveway at Faye's, he continued around a second time.

"What are you doing?" I asked.

"Do you really want to stay here?" he asked slyly, not taking his eyes off the road.

"Where else would I go?" I replied, knowing full well that Marian and Bill could not be imposed upon again. "Besides, there's company here now that Faye's back from her leave."

"I think you should come home with me," Jack ventured, continuing to drive slowly around Tewodros Square.

I was to find out that life decisions can be made in the wink of an eye, or perhaps more to the point, in the short distance of a roundabout. I went home with Jack, and never left.

At first I was a curiosity, a source of gossip for the building staff, who maintained a lively social life amid their own small rooms on the roof. Neighbors, particularly several Greek families who lived in the white building across the street, would peer off their balconies as Jack and I came and went. To my surprise the Shelemay family took me in warmly without a raised eyebrow, Alicia quietly congratulating us on plans still to be determined. Suddenly, I lived on Benin Sefer.

I spent nearly three weeks in Addis Ababa, attending to miscellaneous business and a futile search for effective repair of my tape recorder. With little organized activity and the Addis Ababa restaurants no longer a mystery, Jack and I spent quiet evenings at home together, testing the relationship we had begun to build during my prior stay in the capital. We began to make plans, talking about the possibility of traveling together in Ethiopia, where we might document Ethiopian music and dance on videotape or film. Initially I was concerned that the newness of Ethiopia and the strain of fieldwork might be subtly influencing me to seek reassurance and attachment. But both my head and my heart were already engaged by a new world that had opened with a quickness and depth that took my breath away.

Slowly, too, I began to learn more about the Shelemay family history and the extraordinary events that had brought the family to Ethiopia from Aden. No one knew exactly when their ancestors had arrived in Aden following the exile of Jews from Spain, but the family had certainly lived in southern Arabia since at least the eighteenth century. Jack's mother, Miriam, was a vigorous woman with brown hair and beautiful hazel eyes flecked with gray. She was barely eighteen when she married Shalom Shelemay in 1920. He was several years older, a well-built man with the large eyes that all of his children inherited.

Shalom Shelemay first worked as a clerk and draftsman, but in a few years struck out on his own into the textile trade. He imported linen, silk, and cotton twills from Europe and sold them in Aden and other ports in the nearby Horn of Africa. He would leave Aden for several months at a time, first traveling to Italy to purchase goods, then returning to sail from port to port in wooden dhows. His local itinerary would be determined by the winds that blew across the Gulf of Aden and the Red Sea. He sailed to Djibouti and also frequented Barberra, the Somali port, from where he could take a train to Ethiopia, stopping to trade at Diredawa. He often went to Addis Ababa and in 1940 set up a small office in the Ethiopian capital.

As the business prospered, the Shelemay family grew. In 1945 many of the ten Shelemay children were still living in a large house overlooking the city gardens along the sea in Aden. The building had a lower floor of granite and upper stories of whitewashed limestone to insulate against the heat. On the ground floor was a tobacco factory where Camel cigarettes were made. A broad staircase led up to the second floor, where a large door opened into the Shelemay dwelling.

The home reflected the international nature of Aden—uncurtained floor-to-ceiling Venetian-style windows lighted a room furnished with cane armchairs fitted with upholstered pillows. Scattered around were carved Indian tables inlaid with ivory. Ceiling fans made a soft hum as they circulated the hot desert air. Black-and-white tiled floors led through a door to a veranda running the length of the house, facing the public gardens and beyond them the sea.

Only the parents had a permanent bedroom with European-style beds. The children migrated with the seasons, sleeping on cotton-filled futons set out nightly. Usually the roof was their dormitory. The voice of the sea and the whoosh of wind in the trees were broken at dawn by the sounds of Bedouins leading camel trains, each beast struggling under a load of two huge bags of charcoal for neighborhood households.

With Aden under British protection, the trauma of World War II touched it only peripherally. Families would gather on their roofs to watch occasional dogfights between British and Italian planes over the sea. Sometimes a siren would sound and residents would bring out gas masks issued by the authorities in preparation for an attack that never came. Shalom served as a warden for civil defense, attending periodic drills on the local soccer field with several of his young sons trailing behind.

By the late 1940s, the five older Shelemay children were adults moving into their own worlds—Salamone and Ben into business with their father, Mary to her own home at eighteen in an arranged marriage, Suzanne and Margaret completing their studies at a local convent school run by Irish nuns living in this outpost of the British Empire.

The five younger children included a trio of sons born in sequence between 1935 and 1938. Moshe was the eldest, a fun-loving, good-natured boy, followed by Jack, and then slight, quiet Danny. At the age of four each boy began to attend a traditional Jewish boys' school in the morning, extending his studies when he was six to include secular subjects and lessons in English and Arabic. After school a learned Yemenite teacher, called a *mori*, tutored the three boys in studies of the *Talmud*. When the day's studies were completed, the boys would often, accompanied by their father, board a bus bound for Steamer Point, the harbor area where ships passing to and from the Orient stopped to refuel and unload cargo. Amid the bustle of duty-free shops, hotels, and bars, Moshe, Jack, and Danny would be treated to ice cream before sunset dictated the return home.

Life was quiet in the years after World War II and the Jews of Aden prospered, living in their own neighborhood, buffered from Moslem areas by Indian families living in between. But in the late fall of 1947 the United Nations voted to establish a Jewish state in Palestine. The outbreak of hostilities in what soon would become the state of Israel had an unexpected impact.

The news caused turmoil throughout the Arab Near East. One morning several days after the vote, gangs began roaming the streets of Aden's Jewish quarter, stoning homes and anyone unfortunate enough to be caught in the open. The tension escalated and the mobs began to set fire to buildings on main streets in the area. The tobacco factory below the Shelemay house made an attractive target and young Jack, sitting on the floor next to the apartment door, suddenly smelled kerosene and felt a surge of heat. He screamed an alarm to the family, who fled to the roof, all other exits blocked by fire and the raging mob below.

Cautiously peering down into the street, the family could see Moslem soldiers shooting at Jews trying to escape the mob and the flames. A young housemaid trying to water down red-hot iron girders on the roof of the neighboring building suddenly fell, mortally wounded by a bullet.

With no time to spare the family made a bridge, out of several discarded wooden planks, that barely spanned the narrow alley separating them from the next block of houses. They carefully crossed and turned back to see their house erupt in flames.

The Shelemays made their way to a nearby relative's house where they took refuge during three more days of rioting. Eventually British troops arrived to quell the disturbance, and the family went to Miriam's mother's home where they passed a difficult year. Upon receiving new British passports they left Aden for Addis Ababa, moving into a small house in the courtyard under what was to become the Addis Ababa synagogue on Benin Sefer.

In the quarter-century since their final move to Ethiopia, the family had become a virtual institution in the country. The compound on Benin Sefer was constructed with the enthusiastic support of Emperor Haile Selassie, who drove by several times a week to inspect what was, in the early 1950s, the tallest building in the Ethiopian capital.

Benin Sefer became a microcosm of Ethiopian diversity: at the top of the hill was the synagogue; at the bottom, a mosque. Five times a day the sounds of the *muezzin* chanting prayers from the minaret washed over the Shelemay compound, in counterpoint, on Sundays and holidays, with the bells of the many Ethiopian Orthodox churches in the capital.

So the Shelemays, and the other Adenite families who had arrived at the same time, built a new and prosperous life in Ethiopia. They became an integral part of an already large foreign community in the capital. Jews, Armenians, Indians, Italians, Greeks—groups of these nationalities made Ethiopia their home and brought with them a variety of skills in commerce and industry.

Apart from a safe haven, Ethiopia offered almost unlimited business opportunities. Few Ethiopians were involved in commercial affairs and the expertise of foreigners was needed. If this country never openly invited outsiders, certainly Ethiopians tolerated the presence of the foreign community; there grew an increasingly symbiotic relationship. Over the years the permanent foreign and diplomatic communities became intertwined with each other, and with the Ethiopian officials and aristocracy needed to help open doors. The cosmopolitan nature of the capital also grew over the years, particularly with the establishment of the Organization of African Unity in Addis Ababa, making Ethiopia host to a sophisticated diplomatic community from every corner of the globe.

Among the permanent residents, each nationality tended to specialize in certain trades or professions. Many Indians were teachers and shopkeepers, or traders, like a number of Greek residents. Most of the Italians worked as repairmen, truckers, and builders. The Armenians were printers, jewelers, and shopowners. With an emperor anxious to bring his country into the twentieth century and a history largely free of the colonial experience that had scarred most of the rest of Africa, Ethiopia nurtured its permanent foreign community. There was little animosity even toward the Italian invaders, many of whom returned to Ethiopia after the war, married Ethiopian women, and made the country their adopted home.

In return for their security these individuals made a commitment to the country, building homes and helping to establish medical and cultural facilities. Many adopted the Ethiopian citizenship offered by the emperor in his attempt to integrate them more fully into Ethiopian life.

The Shelemays declined to take Ethiopian citizenship and retained their British passports acquired in Aden. When asked about the future Shalom would reply, "We are only temporarily here, my dear." Perhaps the traumatic events in Aden remained too powerful a memory, or perhaps it was the concern that someday tragedy could threaten Ethiopia itself. Once, during an attempted coup in 1960, the family had experienced days of terror. With tanks stationed at strategic points in the city and rumors of a coup circulating, they closed their offices and returned home, at that time a large villa located in Casa Populare, a residential zone built by Italians in the southern part of the capital.

On one side of the villa, at some distance, was an Ethiopian army camp; on the other were the offices of the American Military Advisory and Assistance Group. Suddenly, in the middle of lunch, bullets began flying through the Shelemay house. The family spent three days huddled in inner rooms as small arms fire intermittently swept the area. Only when the coup was declared unsuccessful, when the emperor had regained power, did the shooting stop. The Shelemays later asked the soldiers from the camp what they had been shooting at and were told that, in fact, the soldiers were not sure.

Despite such sobering experiences, the foreign community was largely complacent about its future. No matter what happened to the emperor, they thought, Ethiopia would remain a strong ally of the West. All knew that, whether they had become naturalized Ethiopians or not, they were always *ferenj*. But to be called a *ferenj* was not an insult—it was a way of life.

During the time I spent in Addis Ababa with Jack after my first period of fieldwork in the north, I worked during the day at his apartment, transcribing my field tapes and analyzing what I had gathered so far. Sometimes I'd stop and write a letter home to my parents in Texas, looking up at the filmy lace curtains blowing in the breeze next to the terrace door, wondering how much to share of this strange new life. I was overwhelmed at the changes enveloping me and my future. So quickly my research trip had taken on a new dimension.

Often I would walk in the family's garden, a haven from the sounds and smells of urban Ethiopia. Hidden from the street behind the white building, it contrasted strikingly with a neglected tennis court, littered with a few discarded tires and occupied by two sad-eyed cows, adjacent to it.

The garden held an abundance of French hybrid roses, flowering trees, snapdragons, daffodils, and lilies, all of which could be admired from small, well-trimmed paths. A swing hung from a tree near the papyrus that grew alongside an old well. One large plot in the back was left unplanted, intended only for Salamone's use as a place to slaughter cows or sheep, according to Jewish law, for the family. In this garden refuge I often sat under the fir and eucalyptus trees that shaded the high stone wall at the rear of the compound, trying to assimilate all that was happening to me.

One weekend Jack and I drove west to the Awash game preserve, a grassy flatland studded with lava fields from once-active volcanos in the area and crossed by the Awash River in its deep gorge. Oryx, ostriches, and kudus roamed the golden plains, their domain invaded only occasionally by parties of Danakil nomads who resented the loss of prime grazing land for outsiders' pleasure.

We spent two nights in a small camp of metal trailers intended to house visitors until a hotel could be built. It was in the Awash, one lazy afternoon, that we decided to share a future.

I was not anxious to leave Jack but I wanted to participate in an important Beta Israel religious pilgrimage in early November, and that was fast approaching. I realized that I now had an opportunity to expand my project and do long-term research in Beta Israel villages. I left again for Gondar, this time with a round-trip airplane ticket, from Jack, in my bag.

5

MONKS AND MISSIONARIES

I returned to Gondar, where I had quickly located a place to stay during my first trip north. Two young Frenchmen lived in a house just off the main road into town and had an empty bedroom they were willing to rent. The simple villa was most notable for its erratic water supply, but it did have one redeeming feature—a front porch with a lovely view of the green, rolling mountains and a small, round Ethiopian Church in the distance.

Pierre and Jean worked in agricultural development, jobs they had chosen as an alternative to military service in France. They were taciturn if pleasant companions, glad to have a third person to share the modest expenses of the house, including the salary of a young Ethiopian girl named Mizraq who cleaned and cooked an occasional meal.

Adjacent to our house was a large, fenced compound where one of the doctors from the Gondar public health school and hospital lived. Dr. Giyorgis had studied medicine in Europe and was on cordial terms with Pierre and Jean. When he heard about my return to Gondar and the latest developments in my romance with Jack, he quickly volunteered that I should make my regular collect telephone calls from his house, rather than from the public phone in the Gondar Post Office. My communications with Jack had already become a source of great amusement among the Gondar operators, who during my earlier stay had often mimicked our endearments to each other when I placed my calls. "I love you, Mrs. Kay," once giggled a particularly cheeky operator as I waited for my connection.

On days when I was not in the villages Gondar offered numerous diversions. One could ride a *gari*, a horse-drawn cart that served as a local taxi, up the curving road into town to pick up supplies, collect mail, or visit the market. I began to explore the active Gondari musical life, recording a fine local *masenqo* player named Desta who played many highland folksongs, including the ubiquitous love song, *tezzeta*. I discovered that an ensemble of flute players was kept on the municipal payroll so that it would be available for all state occasions. Sometimes I'd go to one of the famous churches of the area. Debre Berhan Selassie, founded by Emperor Iyasu I in the eighteenth century and rebuilt in the nineteenth, quickly became my favorite—paintings of countless angels' faces filled its ceiling, where they appeared to hover, gazing down on the faithful below.

Often I tried to talk to Mizraq, who would giggle as she answered my questions and then slip away. Once she disappeared for a few days without explanation, afterward saying only that she had been ill. A couple of weeks later I was appalled to find out from neighbors that she had suffered a miscarriage, the loss of a pregnancy of which we were unaware. I told Mizraq that I was sorry to hear about the loss of her baby, and she answered quietly, "It is nothing," accepting her misfortune without further comment.

It felt good to return to Ambober on a clear, sunny morning in mid-November, several days before the *Seged*, a pilgrimage and feast celebrated by the Beta Israel once a year. Dragonflies buzzed about the bushes and tall grass. Workmen from Gondar were raising the wooden frame for a new school building alongside the old stone structure, shattering the village quiet with hammering and loud conversation. Villagers seemed to be moving about more than usual, women grinding grain for the bread needed to feed the many friends and relatives expected from neighboring villages.

Barely had I stashed my things into a corner of the old schoolhouse office when I heard a familiar voice calling out to me in English. I turned to see Yosef Berhanu, an elder of the community, standing at the schoolhouse door. He had arrived the previous day from Addis Ababa for the *Seged*.

A man in his sixties, Yosef had grown up in a village that now no longer existed, that was deserted when its residents were forced to relocate to Ambober during the Italian occupation of 1936. Yosef was born into the changing Falasha world of the teens and twenties, when the first regular contacts with Jews from abroad were beginning to reshape Beta Israel traditions and identities. With the permission of his parents he was one of the teenagers sent to Europe for education by Jacques Faitlovitch. Yosef spent years abroad in Germany and then Palestine, learning German, Hebrew, and English, and studying fundamentals of Jewish history, religious law, and liturgy. He returned to Ethiopia determined to devote his life to making his community part of the Jewish mainstream.

After the Italian occupation, which brought the deaths of so many of Ethiopia's intelligentsia, Yosef was named an official of the Ministry of Education. Now a permanent resident of Addis Ababa, he had served increasingly over the years as the unofficial Falasha tie to the outside world. His fluency in languages made him an ideal contact for individuals who wished information about the community, while his honesty and straightforward manner rendered him the natural conduit for those who sought to send it aid.

Yosef was a scholar who kept on the shelf in his modest living room in Addis Ababa a small collection of books written about his people by others—Faitlovitch's description in German of his first trip to the Falasha, Aescoly's classic study in Hebrew, and Wolf Leslau's translation of Falasha literary texts, the *Falasha Anthology*. Yosef himself had published an annotated Hebrew calendar transliterated into Amharic that had been distributed in the villages. But closest to his heart was an Amharic-Hebrew dictionary on which he had worked for twenty years, compiling each entry on a card and then painstakingly entering them by hand on large white sheets of paper bound together in a worn leather cover.

Yosef and I had met many times before, both in Israel and in Addis Ababa. He had contacted the priests and teachers in advance of my first arrival in Ambober, smoothing my entry into the village. I rushed to greet him. This stately, white-haired man always wore Western suits, but now he was dressed for the first time in my memory in a traditional Ethiopian *shamma* draped over a white shirt and jodphurs. He told me that all the priests were away from the village that day or otherwise occupied, so there would be no daily prayer service that evening. Disappointed, I nonetheless accepted his invitation to accompany him to the house of Dawit, a soft-spoken villager who had attended school in Gondar and had trained afterward as a dresser under a foreign physician who had lived briefly in the area.

We followed the main village path to the clinic, which Dawit showed to me with great pride. Housed in a tiny, one-room building with a metal roof, the clinic contained a desk, a wooden examining table, and a simple cupboard of supplies and basic first aid equipment. Any serious problems would have to be handled at the mission clinic, which was staffed with a nurse, just over the hill at Macha. True emergencies required transport to the hospital attached to the public health school in Gondar.

The dusty compound was surrounded by a vine-laced wooden fence; we walked across and sat in the fading afternoon light at the entrance to Dawit's house. Over strong Ethiopian coffee and local *araqi* liquor we recounted our various routes of arrival to the north from the capital and discussed the plans for the upcoming *Seged*. Dawit brought out a radio and all gathered around to hear the evening news broadast. As twilight fell, Dawit's family and guests began to prepare for night in the two-room house, covering metal cots in the front room with rough mattresses.

Accompanied by Dawit's young son I made my way back to the school, where the superintendent's office now became my bedroom. I lit a sterno and heated up a can of corn and tomato soup that warmed me against the evening chill. After a last trip to the outhouse, I secured the bent metal door and left the room in inky darkness. I climbed into my sleeping bag, arranged somewhat precariously on the sturdy table in the center of the room. One night on the rough dirt floor had sent me to this higher perch, in hopes of avoiding spiders and whatever else might choose to make its nocturnal rounds. With a last pass of my flashlight around the room, I was enveloped by a dark silence broken only by the squealing cries of wild dogs that roamed the countryside at night.

There was again no prayer service the next morning, but Yosef stopped by the school to suggest that we walk up the large hill adjoining the village and view the site where the *Seged* would be held the following day. I eagerly agreed, and we set out. A winding path led around the side of the schoolhouse, then beyond the confines of the village. After crossing an open, level pasture, it began to narrow and ascend. The increasingly rough path had been worn up the side of a hill immediately before us; it was shaded only occasionally by trees clinging to the steep slope. At the summit we could look down on Ambober and other villages scattered over the mountainsides, in the area known as Seramle. On this clear day Gondar could be seen faintly in the distance to the northwest.

Continuing our walk across a level clearing at the top of the hill, we could see evidence of *Seged* past. On a small rise in the otherwise level summit was a grove of eucalyptus trees, set apart by a low wall of large stones piled one atop the other, ringing the trunks like a choker. "This is a clean place," remarked Yosef, "a place without graves, which is necessary to hold the *Seged* ceremony." I thought to myself of the other Agau peoples of the area who observed ceremonies in groves of trees on hillsides and wondered if some part of that heritage was still maintained by the Falasha.

During the days that followed Yosef and the priests of Ambober and surrounding villages told me about the meaning of the holiday. Each emphasized a different aspect. It was no wonder that other researchers had been confused or unclear about its significance—*Seged* had at least five layers of meaning that I could discern.

By 1973, *Seged* had become primarily a day when clergy and

individuals from different villages in the region could come together to pray, to feast, and to assert religious and communal soli-
darity. Each Falasha area had its own clean place, its own *Seged*
mountain, where the local community could ascend to pray.
The ascent up the mountain and the ritual which included the
reading of the Ten Commandments, led many, including Yosef,
to compare the *Seged* mountain to Mount Sinai, and to view the
ceremony as an affirmation of the bond between the Beta Israel
and God. Apart from the Decalogue, the readings for the day
included sections of the books of Nehemiah and Jeremiah. Especially noted by all the priests was the reading of Jeremiah's prohibition against marriage to Babylonian wives. Given the strong
Beta Israel taboo against marriage outside their own community,
this passage must have had special meaning to those who read it
aloud and then translated it into Amharic for the entire group.
The *Seged* day was celebrated as a partial fast: all refrained from
food or drink until after the descent from the mountain in mid-
afternoon. This fast signaled *Seged*'s significance as a day of repentance, and many still called the day *Mehella*, a word of forgotten
meaning but one associated with the occasional days of penitence
celebrated by Ethiopian Christians. Many older villagers climbed
the *Seged* mountain with small stones held on their shoulders or
upon their heads in a well-known Ethiopian sign of contrition.
When they reached the top of the mountain both men and
women would bow low, touching their foreheads to the ground.
This motion must have been a longtime part of the ritual since
the opening prayer for the day exclaims, "Come and let us bow
down," and the name of the day, *Seged*, is from a verb meaning
"to bow." Throughout the service, men and women all over the
mountaintop bowed repeatedly.
One of the oldest priests, a wizened, bent man named Seyum
who lived a few minutes' walk from Tadda, mentioned a significance of the holiday not discussed by the others. As he spoke, I remembered having read the same story in the writings of Johannes
Flad, a German missionary who spent time among the Falasha

in the 1860s. According to Seyum, *Seged* had once marked the annual retreat of the Falasha monks, who left their villages for a period of fasting and contemplation each year.

Perhaps no aspect of Beta Israel tradition had been as puzzling to earlier visitors as the fact that the clergy of this community had also included, in addition to the priests and *debtera*, both monks and nuns. By the 1970s, no monks survived in the Falasha villages I visited, though a few elderly anchorites were rumored still to be living up in the Semien Mountains to the north. Of the Falasha nuns almost nothing was remembered beyond a few colorful stories of their self-sacrificing and sometimes miraculous care of sick or injured men and beasts.

Not much more than a quarter-century before, however, many Falasha communities had been witness to a strong monastic presence, with one or more monks living in their own quarters on the edge of each village. These monks lived and ate alone, forbidden by strict laws of purity to share food with others outside their order. They lived simple lives, tilling small gardens and tending honey-producing hives. Young boys who were priests-in-training would serve them, helping to cultivate the crops and to tend household chores.

The monks had been the primary carriers of Falasha liturgical tradition and for centuries were responsible for training priests to perform prayers within the prayerhouse. It was to these monks, one of whom also served as high priest, that a village turned for guidance in religious and daily affairs.

The monks traced their presence among the Beta Israel to the life and impact of Abba Sabra, an Ethiopian Christian monk said to have lived during the reign of Emperor Zar'a Ya'qob in the mid-fifteenth century. According to Beta Israel oral traditions, Abba Sabra had fled his monastery after committing a crime and sought refuge among them. Once settled in his new community, he is said to have organized the Beta Israel prayers and music.

The Beta Israel community prayed twice a day in the prayerhouse, morning and evening, led by priests the monks had trained. In years past the monks sometimes came to the prayerhouse, entering through the east door intended for them alone, an innovation introduced by one of Abba Sabra's successors, Abba Halen. But Abba Sabra himself is said to have instituted the laws of isolation so strictly observed among the Beta Israel, to have taught them about their history, and, finally, to have started the celebration of the *Seged*.

By late in the afternoon before the *Seged*, men, women, and children had begun to arrive from all over the area. They carried parcels wrapped in cloth, baskets holding foodstuffs for the trip. Cries of joy could be heard throughout the village as the many small compounds welcomed relatives and friends, each already crowded hut swelling with the influx.

Early in the morning of the *Seged* ceremony, Priest Mika'el led two brown oxen to the prayerhouse compound where he said an invocation and then slaughtered them according to biblical prescription. He slit their throats quickly with a gleaming metal knife, holding each to allow the blood to trickle away from the body. All parts of the body except the forbidden sinews and muscles were retained, the skin immediately taken away for curing by one of the men of the village.

In the past the Beta Israel had practiced animal sacrifice on important annual holidays, using a special altar of smooth stone set up in the courtyard of every *masgid*. This long-standing tradition existed no more, in part because of the endemic poverty of the Ethiopian countryside, and in part because of the criticism of this practice by outsiders.

In the *Seged*, the oxen met their end to provide meat for an eagerly anticipated feast. Near the place of slaughter young boys built a fire contained within a circle of stones and erected a long wooden spit supported by posts at both ends to hold large pieces of meat for roasting. Several would remain to tend the fire and cook the meat during the long hours of ritual upon the mountain, preparing to greet the hungry congregation with food after their descent.

Around 10 A.M., all four Ambober priests, along with several others from Tadda and the surrounding villages, went into the prayerhouse. For a time they remained within, their preparations hidden from the small group of villagers gathering outside. Then they emerged singing the melody heard at the beginning of every holiday morning service, on this occasion with words heralding the beginning of the *Seged*. Several carried large multicolored umbrellas with swinging fringes. Priest Mika'el carried a drum, the *negarit*, that appeared like a large, flattened wooden salad bowl with a skin stretched across the top.

Priest Ya'qob held a flat metal gong called the *qachel* in one hand and the small metal stick with which it was struck in the other. Accompanying the priests were several young boys, two carrying on their heads the leather-bound manuscripts of the *Orit*, each volume wrapped in a length of decorative cloth. The *Orit* was accorded a place of great honor within the Beta Israel prayerhouse, where it was kept within a small cabinet on the western wall. What was known as the *tabot*, the collective name for the Five Books of Moses, was for the Beta Israel at once both sacred writ and symbol of the covenant with God. A third young boy steadied on his head the minature Hebrew *Torah* scroll, about eighteen inches high, wrapped in the same patterned cloth as the *Orit*.

The procession moved slowly across the pasture and up the path, the priests singing a prayer of thanksgiving as they proceeded. At the top they approached the eucalyptus grove, and Alaqa Gete, the local master of Ge'ez, assumed his place as head priest at the center of the circle of rocks. The other priests moved to positions both within and around the circumference of stones, arranging the Ge'ez manuscripts and the Hebrew *Torah* scroll carefully on the narrow ledge. Finally, Priest Mika'el laid a length of the flowered cloth over the side of the rocks facing the congregation, anchoring the material on the upper ledge with small stones.

After the people had assumed their places, the priests began their prayers, sometimes fading to a faint murmur as strong winds swept the hilltop. Members of the congregation bowed, prayed, talked, even slept, scattered around the summit. Midway through the service the singing stopped, and Alaqa Gete approached the largest *Orit* resting on the stone wall below him. He read the Ten Commandments in Geʻez, pausing while Priest Mikaʼel translated each injunction into Amharic. Afterward, Gete moved back and Yosef slipped through a break in the stones and recited the commandments in Hebrew, answered by the ululation of the women. All the while a young boy held the Hebrew *Torah* scroll aloft.

Following a final hour of prayers the priests yielded again to Yosef, who climbed up within the circle of stones. He spoke at length, seeking to comfort a community distressed by the break in Ethiopian-Israeli relations in the wake of the Yom Kippur War. Yosef made only veiled references to Beta Israel hopes for emigration to Israel, nervous that the several non-Falasha teachers in attendance from the Ambober school might report to local authorities any controversial statements. He concluded his talk with the injunction that, because of the recent conflict in the Middle East, the *Seged* feast should not be celebrated that day in the usual joyous fashion, with music-making and dancing. Individuals should share their food in a sober atmosphere appropriate to these tragic times.

I could not help but note the paradox of a people gathered on an Ethiopian mountaintop to mourn a conflict that had taken place so many miles away. Was their concern about governmental eyes and ears a real one? In recent years the Beta Israel had received aid from organizations and individuals in Israel and the United States, help modest by international standards, but a source of jealousy amid the poverty that surrounded them.

Also on the mountain that day, to my great surprise, were three missionaries from the nearby British mission at Macha. I had not met them before and had been told by individuals in Israel that they were mistrusted by the Falasha of Ambober and Seramle. These comments had reinforced my own already critical opinion of the missions, whose activities, along with those of Western Jews in the area, I regarded as collectively guilty of a century of gross interference in Beta Israel life. Since the beginning of my time in the north I had been polite to those missionaries I encountered, but I had avoided more formal social contact.

But it soon became clear that the people of Ambober did not resent the three gentle British souls who staffed the mission over the hill. Jenny, Harold, and Jill were greeted warmly by many, both men and women shaking their hands and bowing with obvious enthusiasm. Individuals sitting nearby pointed out the visitors to me and related stories of the medical care they had received at the mission clinic. Jenny, a round woman somewhere in mid-life, with curly brown hair, was a nurse respected for her gentle, competent care. Tall, balding Harold oversaw mission religious activities and ran the mission school with the help of freckled Jill, whose lively demeanor and red hair gave evidence of Irish blood. The three were well prepared for the day, dressed in khakis and windbreakers, canteens slung over Harold's left shoulder. In a break between speeches they approached and greeted me warmly, welcoming me to the area.

After several hours the priests completed their prayers. They folded up the ritual cloth and gathered the sacred books for the procession down the hill, once more singing the verses of the first prayer of the ritual, over and over again, as they descended. But once this procession reached the pasture, its atmosphere of penitence and sadness abruptly gave way to revelry.

Several young Falasha students who had arrived home from studies in Gondar ran to the front of the crowd and put on an exhibition of strength, trying to split stones against their bare chests with karate-like motions. Many villagers gathered around, cheering each in his turn. Meanwhile, the priests slowly made their way across the pasture and up the path to the prayerhouse, their restrained chanting giving way to joyous dancing in a circle, accompanied by the *negarit* and the *qachel*.

The crowd moved toward the prayerhouse compound where roasted meat awaited and the young cooks were occupied in a futile effort to ward off the ever-present flies. Large earthenware jars of *tella* sat nearby, pieces of fermented grain floating on its surface. Women produced pottery dishes and baskets to hold their family's portion of the bounty. As more came forth to claim their share of the festive meal three musicians from surrounding villages suddenly arrived and began to bow a popular song in unison on their *masenqo*. Yosef rushed into the prayerhouse, where the priests were still putting away the ritual objects used on the mountaintop. He emerged with Alaqa Gete, who announced in a loud and peremptory tone that everyone should take the food to their own compounds if they desired further revelry and music.

The crowd began to dissipate, each musician moving in the direction of a family group that signaled interest in his services. As the crowd dispersed I was invited along with the Macha missionaries to a nearby house for tea. Over steaming cups, we spoke of the latest local news—a young shepherd had somehow cut his leg badly on a plow and had been taken to the mission for first aid.

Somewhat later, when they were about to say their good-byes, Jenny turned to me and asked if I would like to return for the night to Macha. Weary and short of supplies after several days in the village, I was also a bit homesick, having waked up with a start that morning to realize it was both the tenth anniversary of John F. Kennedy's death and Thanksgiving Day. I accepted their offer and went quickly to gather my things for the ride in their Land Rover to the mission.

Macha was located just over the mountain to the southeast of Ambober, but the steep grade and thick undergrowth made it necessary to take a longer, more circuitous route around the bottom of the ridge. About an hour after we started, we pulled up before the small mission. Ringed by a fence, the compound boasted a whitewashed cottage, surrounded by carefully tended sweet peas and tall white lilies, where the three lived. The mud-walled, tin-roofed school building held a classroom, as well as a larger hall for church services and other gatherings. The clinic was a utilitarian, wooden structure with a new wing, intended to house a pediatric clinic, under construction.

Our first order of business was a bath. After days of splashing well water from a bucket and making surreptitious trips to the outhouse when no children were around to watch, the mission bathroom was a revelation. It housed a real Western toilet with a pull flush and a huge metal tub that was filled with freshly heated water by the mission staff shortly after our arrival. Whether because I was the guest or because I was ripest, I got to use the tub first. I slipped down into the warm water, days of dust and fatigue floating away.

After everyone had bathed we spent that cool November evening in the middle of the Ethiopian highlands eating a traditional English dinner, complete with mincemeat pie and custard. Afterward we sat outside in cane chairs on the simple terrace, looking out into the night. Reluctant to speak about religious activities, Harold mentioned only that their number of converts was small. Jenny talked more freely about the medical services, which she and the others saw as their primary contribution.

The bulk of mission resources were quite obviously devoted to running the clinic. The religious venture appeared no more successful than that of most of the missionaries of the past century, who had experienced limited success in part because they were required to baptize their converts into the Ethiopian Orthodox church. Though it was clear that thousands had left the Beta Israel community and that their number had dwindled to fewer than thirty thousand by the early 1970s, the activity of foreign Christian missionaries accounted for only a small part of the attrition. The more powerful lure was Ethiopian Christianity with its promise of an upward leap of class into the Christian Amhara mainstream.

On the other hand it was clear that the missionaries had made a great contribution to local medical resources. Jenny offered remarkably sophisticated first aid, dispensing antibiotics and other remedies as needed and training local women to carry out simple procedures in a small laboratory partitioned off from the main clinic. She spoke with concern of the distressingly high rate of infant mortality, which had led her to plan to establish a pediatric clinic with the help of a second nurse who was soon to arrive.

Early the next morning, I attended the regular mission prayer meeting led by a Falasha convert in Amharic. Afterward, Jenny showed me around the frame building that housed the clinic. Our tour was suddenly interrupted when we heard cries outside the door; we went out to find two men lowering a makeshift stretcher to the ground. On it lay a woman, the wife of one of the men, obviously in pain and holding a dirty, squalling newborn boy.

Jenny asked what had happened. The woman had been in labor for three days, her husband answered, when they decided to bring her to the clinic. But while they were carrying her, having set out several hours earlier that morning, the baby had suddenly arrived and had fallen out onto the road. Jenny quickly examined the screaming but otherwise healthy infant, securing him in a small basket and handing him over to one of the lab assistants for a wash. She directed the men to carry the woman inside, and then sent them out so that she could examine the mother, who now rested on a padded examining table in the corner of the room.

To Jenny's experienced eye, it was obvious that the afterbirth was almost as slow to be expelled as had been the baby. She suspected that the problem was an overfull bladder. As Jenny assembled catherization equipment, the woman suddenly cried out, not in pain but in fear of the bottles, assorted tubes, and plastic bags now resting on the white metal table beside her. I held her hand while Jenny inserted the catheter and emptied her bladder. Then she massaged the woman's abdomen to force out the recalcitrant placenta.

Later that day Jill drove into Gondar to shop for supplies, dropping me off at my small house on her way into town. Life in Gondar was just as I had left it a few days earlier. I arrived to find a note inviting me to a party that night at the home of our neighbors and word from Jean and Pierre that the weekly news magazines had never arrived at the newsstand, falling victim to the censor for some real or imagined breach of security.

6

MARRIAGE AND REVOLUTION

I returned to Addis Ababa in mid-December, earlier than I had expected. Word had reached Jack's mother, who had lived in Israel since 1967, that Jack finally had a serious girlfriend. Having just emerged from mourning little more than a year after her husband's death, she announced that she would come to Ethiopia for a visit in January to take stock of this startling development. She had no idea that Jack's American friend was already living on Benin Sefer, an arrangement she certainly would have disapproved of had she learned of it. When he got word of the impending visit Jack called to tell her that she should postpone her trip since we would be coming to Israel anyway to get married. So in this manner we decided to have a Tel Aviv wedding in February and to travel to Israel beforehand to make the necessary preparations.

I left Ambober in mid-December with promises that I would be back for the Passover celebration in the spring. Wezero Alganesh, when told of my wedding, began to weave a basket for me as a gift. Such gift baskets, often of a conical shape and made of multicolored woven reeds, are given as a sign of good luck. When we parted, Alganesh promised that I would receive it from her upon my return.

The weeks before our departure from Ethiopia were filled with preparations. Most urgently, everyone concurred, I needed a trousseau. The few dresses I had brought with me were appropriate for neither the Mediterranean winter nor the social events to come. But in Addis Ababa one does not simply enter a shop and pull selections off the rack. The stores that carried European fashions had stock often years out of date, and what they had was priced beyond all reason because of the enormous costs of freight and duty. Aware of the problem, my sister-in-law-to-be, Alicia, immediately took me in hand, perhaps sensing a bond because my decision to become a Shelemay had been made almost as quickly as her own some twenty years before. A sixth-generation Jerusalemite, she had met Jack's eldest brother, Salamone, during one of his trips to Israel in the early 1950s and had abruptly broken off a previous engagement in order to marry him. After the wedding, it took them two weeks to travel from Israel to Ethiopia, an odyssey of rough flights on Dakota airplanes filled with passengers, chickens, and produce, broken by days of waiting for the next connection in Cyprus, Port Sudan, and Eritrea. Alicia's first taste of the expatriate's Africa came at Port Sudan, where she and Salamone spent nearly a week at an elegant British hotel isolated in the desert, a pampered world that contrasted sharply with the poverty all around.

Alicia and Salamone had lived in a wing of the sprawling family villa at Casa Populare until everyone moved into their own apartments in the first Shelemay apartment building on Benin Sefer. In the mid-1960s, when the second Shelemay building was constructed across the street, the triplex on the top floor was designed for them, the master bedroom at the apex of the building opening out onto a deep terrace with views of the city below and the Entoto Mountains in the distance.

An attractive woman in her early forties with short blond hair, Alicia loved the privileged lifestyle of foreign women in the capital. Her days were devoted to running her household and supervising a housemaid and cook, the latter's activities inevitably redirected by Salamone, who often took over duties as chef, leaving only the baking to his wife. Her eldest daughter had left Ethiopia the previous year to attend high school in Israel, but the house was still full with the energy of her lanky twelve-year-old son, Jochanan, who attended the school established for children of the numerous Israeli diplomats and aid officials living in Addis Ababa. With a nurse, called a *mamite*, to care for her youngest, the two-year-old Avi, she was free to socialize and do volunteer work, developing a wide social network that spanned an extraordinary range of nationalities in the foreign community. Fluent in Hebrew, English, French, Spanish, Italian, and Amharic, she possessed almost as wide an array of passports thanks to her French-Moroccan descent, Israeli nationality, and marriage to a British subject.

Her closest friends shared her Middle Eastern background if not her land of birth. Alicia was inseparable from a tall, dark-haired Lebanese woman, who had lived for years with her family in the Ethiopian capital, making a comfortable living as an importer of Italian confectionery and fine French china and silver. Later she was to flee the violence of the Ethiopian revolution with her two teenaged daughters, only to be confronted with another yet more cataclysmic explosion at home in Beirut. A second close friend was a petite, vivacious woman married to a Syrian diplomat. The three used to say, laughing, that their social circle should be a model for a political settlement in the Middle East.

There had been many other friends, too, most drawn from the Israeli diplomatic community. But after the Yom Kippur War that fall and the subsequent break in relations between Israel and Ethiopia, most Israelis abruptly left and their school closed. As I was later to watch her do during the days of anxiety ahead, Alicia simply shrugged off her sadness, transferred her son to the French Lycée, and went on with her life.

The morning after I arrived back in the capital, Alicia called me to come up to her apartment, where we drank camomile tea and leafed through recent copies of *Vogue* and *Cosmopolitan*. "Which designs do you like?" she asked, herself efficiently selecting for me a classic jacket with pants, a dress, and a sleeveless vest and flared skirt. Barely had we finished the tea and Sara Lee cheesecake, the parting gift of an American friend just transferred to another post, when Alicia bustled me down the elevator, across the street, and into her car. We took the quick five-minute drive to the city's main shopping district, the piazza, a section of ramschackle two- and three-story frame buildings with balconies attached along their second stories in an Italianate style. A reminder of the Italian occupation that had begun nearly forty years before, the piazza sat on the rise behind the Municipality Building and was a central location for foreign-owned shops and European merchandise.

"Never walk to the piazza," remarked Alicia as she swerved to avoid a slow-moving donkey and cart immediately in front of us. "The beggars on the street will make it impossible for you to move and someone may try to steal your purse or jewelry." I nodded, not mentioning that I had walked all over Addis Ababa for months, occasionally responding to a child's repeated request for chewing gum or a beggar's plea for change.

We stopped in front of a small shop owned by the Aharonees, an Adenite family that occupied the apartment next door to Alicia in the Shelemay building. The white-haired Aharonee patriarch, Menachem, and his wife, Esther, had lived for years in Asmara, the Italian-built capital of Eritrea. They had moved to Addis Ababa in the mid-1950s to take advantage of better business opportunities but continued to speak Italian and in every way maintain the world of Italian culture to which they were long accustomed.

Their shop seemed to overflow with bolts of colorful silk and wool fabrics imported from the Far East and Europe. After a few minutes of informal conversation over the mandatory cups of Ethiopian coffee, we selected a muted pink-and-beige wool for the dress, a bright red tartan plaid for the vest and skirt, and gray-checked flannel for the pantsuit, buying just enough of each for the designs Alicia had selected.

Next, we delivered the materials to Nella, an Italian dressmaker who lived in a small apartment less than a block away. With dispatch the petite seamstress took my measurements, looked carefully at the magazine pictures, and set her price for a rush order to be finished in less than two weeks.

With a basic wardrobe underway, we went next to a shop of Italian imports, Ariston, owned by yet another Adenite family. Related to the Aharonees, the Banins too were most comfortable speaking Italian after years in Asmara. I immediately liked Esther Banin, a soft-spoken woman with wavy dark hair. First we looked through the racks where each item was kept carefully covered in a plastic garment bag to protect it from dust. With a little coaching I chose a simple brown wool suit and a flowing navy evening gown, both of which Alicia insisted I acquire for the many social events beginning to crowd our calendar. But one most important choice remained—the wedding dress. Esther brought out books of wedding dress designs, any of which, she advised me in halting English, Ariston could reproduce.

"I really don't want a traditional wedding dress," I replied with some trepidation. "In fact, Jack bought me a wonderful long dress of bright flowered organza that I would love to wear for the wedding."

Esther and Alicia looked at each other, and then at me. "You must have a white dress for the wedding," said Alicia firmly. "See if you like one of the designs here."

We picked a long, slim gown to be made of ivory crepe, its simplicity broken only by elaborate beading extending across both shoulders and from the wrist up nearly to the elbow. The wide belt had a buckle encrusted with tiny pearls, the same as those on each of the numerous buttons closing the dress from neckline to hem. Despite my objections, Alicia and Esther insisted that I needed a veil as well, and together they sketched one anchored with a wide band covered with the same fine beading. The dress and veil would be made in Asmara, where tailors did all the work by hand—the gown would be sent back and forth by air for fittings.

I was grateful for the care and help offered by Alicia and the two Esthers. We headed home, and I let myself into Jack's apartment, realizing that it would soon be my own. I made a cup of tea and walked up the wooden staircase to the room that was to be my study. Stacks of books were piled along one long wall while a small sofa sat opposite on the other. The rectangular room was bounded on one end by doors leading out to a terrace. I sat down and stared at the beautiful Persian carpet covered with figures of musicians, brought back from Iran by Jack's sister Aviva but left with him for safekeeping at some point and never reclaimed. Jack had told me that some German friends were about to leave the country and wanted to sell a fine walnut desk, perfect for my study. There I sat, feeling as disordered as the room, lost in uncharted territory.

I had been prepared to feel inadequate as an ethnomusicologist among the Beta Israel. But now I was even more disconcerted than I had been in the countryside, where it was simply assumed that I was completely unfamiliar with virtually everything I encountered.

In Addis Ababa, among a community with whom I shared aspects of religious background and Western culture, it was expected that I should know what to do and what to say. The differences, however, were more formidable than I had at first realized. Though I could communicate with family members easily in English and adequately in Hebrew, and though at home they usually made an effort to speak English when I was around, their conversations would often include phrases in the Judeo-Arabic dialect they had spoken from childhood. In social situations English was rarely the main language. The majority of the Adenite community, who had spent years in Eritrea before coming to Addis Ababa, were most comfortable using Italian, although most knew Amharic as well as Tigrinya, the native language of that northern region. Other Shelemay friends from the international diplomatic community tended to speak French or Spanish. I found myself most at ease with Ethiopian visitors, most of whom knew English as a second language and who, once aware of my interest in Ethiopia and my basic familiarity with Amharic, took pains to explain their language's frequent double entendres. I was overwhelmed at the linguistic facility demonstrated by Jack and his family and was self-conscious about my own shortcomings in this area. In social situations I often had no alternative but polite silence.

Although our shared Jewish background had removed formal barriers to my smooth incorporation into the Shelemay family and the larger Adenite community, the Sephardic rites of their synagogue were, particularly in their musical content, unfamiliar. Many life-cycle customs were new to me, both because of cross-cultural difference and my own lack of religious education in these areas. As a woman I was simply assumed to be knowledgeable about domestic traditions ranging from holiday observance to cuisine. My ignorance often proved embarrassing.

During my first stay in Jack's apartment, after my initial trip to Gondar, I had been treated like a guest. My days had been my own, devoted to working with my tapes and field notes, attending to necessary business, and meeting with other scholars. I certainly enjoyed the new creature comforts available on Benin Sefer, a welcome departure from fending for myself. Even in urban Ethiopia the simplest aspects of everyday life often required enormous amounts of time and energy. Personal necessities such as laundry, shopping, and food preparation were extraordinarily time-consuming. Clothes had to be washed by hand, all vegetables carefully disinfected before use, and water boiled for at least twenty minutes to sterilize it at that high altitude. Although life in the Shelemay compound was not ostentatious, I could not help but notice the striking and often unsettling contrast between our comfort and the deep poverty all around. But I also quickly realized that, with my basic physical needs taken care of, I would have much more time to devote to my work.

When I returned to Addis Ababa in December to prepare for the wedding trip, I became aware almost immediately that my status had changed. I was no longer just the visiting researcher or the girlfriend of one of the more prominent bachelors. A growing number of people in both the foreign and Ethiopian communities now identified me with and as a Shelemay. Mellashu, our housemaid, began to call me "Mrs. Kay" and to look to me for direction in the house. I now had to manage an additional new role as a woman in the permanent expatriate community.

Slowly, I came to make a series of decisions that would enable me to function within this new context while preserving my own independence. On relatively minor items, like the wedding dress, I simply went along with convention. Other issues caused me greater conflict, none more than whether or not to change my name after marriage. I had always felt strongly that women should retain their own names as a symbol of their independence and I was in fact impressed that Ethiopian women actually did so as a matter of tradition. Yet I found myself marrying into a heavily patriarchal family in which great pride was attached to bearing the Shelemay name. To have declined to take his name, although understandable to Jack, would have shocked the rest of his family and the community at large. I already led an unconventional life by the standards of my in-laws, and I planned to continue my career as a researcher and scholar. To have signaled my independence by refusing the Shelemay name would have been unnecessarily provocative and self-defeating.

Jack and I began to spend more time with the family, joining Salamone and Alicia some weekday evenings for homemade pizza, going out together on Sunday evenings to a small Italian restaurant, and receiving invitations from others in the community. Alicia frequently invited me up for tea and cakes so that I could meet the women in her wide social circle. I would reluctantly put away my work, take off my jeans, and put on something more presentable to meet Alicia's fashionably dressed friends. A few times, I sat to one side as they played bridge, one or the other instructing me on the strategy of the game.

My new navy gown made its first appearance at the New Year's Eve party given by the Aharonees to ring in 1974. After a formal, multicourse Italian meal, the twenty-five guests descended to the living room to play remmy, a card game similar to gin rummy. Winners at each table received prizes—small embroidered linen doilies imported from the Far East—and then played each other in a final competition for the grand prize, a handmade Chinese tablecloth. At midnight, everyone drank champagne, unknowingly toasting in a year that would turn their lives upside down.

There were comfortable, leisurely routines established, I was to find out. The Shelemays opened their offices around 9:00 A.M., when the office guard Telaye swept the sidewalk in preparation for the day. The lunch hour stretched from 1:00 until 3:00 P.M., with offices closed while everyone ate a hearty meal before taking a short rest. Since Jack did not have his own cook we ate lunch at Salamone's house, usually returning to our own apartment for a game of Scrabble afterward. Office hours rarely extended beyond 6:00 p.m. Sometimes, around dusk, we took a short ride to the Addis Ababa Hilton, where we would have a drink and look out at the beautifully landscaped grounds.

Much of life was centered in the family compound, with an occasional Sunday picnic in the garden, and, for the men, attendance at the synagogue service on Saturday morning. Like many in the foreign community we had a membership in the Addis Ababa Hilton Club, where hundreds congregated on weekends for swimming and tennis. Our apartment building on Benin Sefer felt almost like a dormitory, each apartment in some measure an extension of the next, and there were moments when each of us might have preferred more privacy. But later, during the many evenings with early curfews, we would be grateful for this proximity and move from apartment to apartment, relieved not to be condemned to the isolation of those living in their own villas. On balance, most seemed to have enjoyed the congenial atmosphere for years, with someone almost always available to supply a missing cooking ingredient or companionship.

In addition to Alicia and Salamone, and the Aharonees next door to them, the building was largely filled with family and friends. Down the hall from Salamone lived one of the daughters of the Aharonees, married to a long-time French resident of Ethiopia who had converted to Judaism. Ella was a beautiful young woman with ivory skin and dark, shoulder-length hair. Her three-year-old daughter, Jacqueline, had become attached to Alicia's younger son, Avi, and could often be seen pulling him around the garden in a wagon and chattering to him in French, which he did not yet understand.

One level below Salamone, and one above us, was the apartment of Moshe, one of the brothers with whom Jack had shared years at a Brighton boarding school. A lively and fun-loving personality, Moshe and his Israeli wife, Yona, lived on the uphill side of the building where the lot thinned; this accounted for the extraordinary shape of their bedroom, which narrowed to a point at one end. Their apartment, originally designed by the architect for his own use, was a multidimensional wonder, each level in some way abutting another, with the living room on the middle level looking through a cutaway in the ivy-covered wall into a sunken dining room below. The youngest Shelemay son, Danny, quiet and shy, lived in a studio apartment filled with books. His sister Aviva, a delicate, dark beauty, also had her own flat. Eight of the fourteen apartments were thus occupied by members of the family or close friends, the rest by foreigners associated with various embassies or international business concerns.

Life was leisurely and secure in late 1973 and early 1974, comfortable at home and at work. Ethiopia seemed the safe haven it had been for decades. Most of the Adenite and other foreign residents prospered and put aside nagging doubts about the future of an empire with an aging emperor at its helm. The signs of impending change were there but were so subtle that only in retrospect could they be seen for what they were to become.

The week before our departure for Israel in early January, an African Studies Conference was held at the Organization for African Unity in Addis Ababa. The emperor, always anxious to assert Ethiopia's leadership role in Africa, had graciously invited the international contingent of scholars to lunch. As a participant I could hardly contain my excitement. Lunch at the palace, like almost everything that had happened that magical fall, seemed a dream.

My colleague Marilyn had also returned to Addis Ababa and together we made our way to the meeting place outside the palace, where, with our invitations, we were to gain entry at midday. Little did anyone suspect that this would be one of the last public events hosted by the emperor.

His Imperial Majesty lived a short distance south of the old Menelik Palace in a sprawling neobaroque stone building constructed in honor of his silver anniversary on the throne. This grand "Jubilee Palace" was protected by the imperial bodyguards, each dressed in olive-brown pants and tunic with a khaki helmet decorated with tufts from a lion's mane. The emperor lived in a luxurious setting that contrasted sharply with the lives of his subjects, most of whom were largely concerned with basic subsistence. In one corner of the manicured grounds, a Japanese rock garden was crossed by a bridge with water coursing underneath it. Peacocks roamed the formal gardens, which were watered and in bloom even in the middle of the Ethiopian dry season. Here and there romped a tiny cheetah or lion cub.

We congregated outside the main gate of the palace, where each of the invitations was carefully scrutinized. After entering the palace grounds, the group of scholars was led through an imposing entrance and along a hall into a mirrored chamber with high ceilings. There, upon a platform at the far end of the room, perched the diminutive emperor, looking somehow lost within the expanse of his ornate chair.

We were welcomed by a member of the emperor's cabinet, and then, in single file, we proceeded slowly to a spot in front of the stairs at the bottom of the platform. Our names were recited to the seemingly attentive emperor. It came my turn and I curtsied, looking up at the end to see a faint smile on that wrinkled face so familiar from photographs. The emperor nodded to each of us as we turned away and proceeded in line down the opposite side of the room and out the door. Members of the imperial bodyguard led us through a series of corridors into a vast dining room.

Lunch proved to be a multicourse banquet. The room was nearly filled with long, wide tables, each running perpendicular to a grand head table set on a dais at one end of the hall. A widower since the death of Empress Menen more than a decade before, the emperor eventually entered the room to our applause, flanked by several of his daughters and granddaughters, all of whom, within the year, would languish in cells within the former emperor Menelik's palace.

The tables were covered with fine white linen and laid with china decorated with the imperial seal. The reason for the unusual number of crystal wine glasses at each place became clear as they were filled, one by one, with the French wine selected to complement each of the five courses. The meal combined the best in European and Ethiopian cuisine, characteristic of an emperor who had long tried to bring the amenities of the West into one of the poorest countries in the world.

The meal ended with a toast, everyone raising glasses of imperial *tedj*, or mead. The emperor, speaking in French, wished us success in our deliberations and an enjoyable stay in Ethiopia. A visiting African scholar rose to give a response. "We wish that all your people may eat as well as we have today," he said loudly, glass raised. A collective gasp broke the hush, most of us startled at this none-too-subtle reference, however appropriate, to the rumored famine in the north. In the stunned silence that followed the emperor slowly rose and led the imperial party away from the head table and out of the room. We finished our *tedj* and were escorted out of the Jubilee Palace, full with drink, still talking about a statement that certainly would have cost an Ethiopian his or her freedom.

Jack and I were married in Tel Aviv on February 4, in a private ceremony for our immediate families performed by a red-haired, bearded rabbi who had joined other Shelemays before us. The wedding came close to never happening because of the strict Israeli laws that require both partners to prove their Jewish background before receiving approval to marry. I had a letter from the brother of the chief rabbi of England, who by coincidence lived near my family in Texas. His name was well known to the panel of venerable rabbis processing our application and my own status was quickly certified. But Jack had only a letter from the secretary of the Jewish community of Addis Ababa, who happened to be his brother, Salamone, and the panel refused his request, despite his parent's longtime residency in Israel. They ordered him to appear before the rabbinical court two days later, where, with the help of an assortment of relatives and friends who vouched for his legitimate descent, we received permission to marry.

Although I was overjoyed by the prospect of a future with Jack, the many hurdles that foreigners must overcome in order to receive permission to marry in Israel required a measure of patience that I found difficult to muster. At first I tried to approach the often frustrating process of planning the wedding in Israel as if I were once again an observer. But my ability to objectify the experience soon collapsed—I could not step back and watch myself like an actress in a play.

In the Beta Israel villages I had been able to accept whatever role I needed to play, at times even enjoying my strange life as a marginal male. I had also begun to negotiate my own distinctive path among the foreign women in Addis Ababa. But as I sat down to discuss my menstrual cycle with a female official at the Israeli rabbinate so that my wedding date could be set without violating Jewish laws of family purity, I felt confused and resentful, overloaded with the multiple situations to which I had to adjust.

In the villages I had been careful not to compromise Beta Israel laws of purity; I never went to these places while menstruating. But the formal acknowledgment of my own ritual impurity in Israel was somehow much more painful; there I was left with the feeling that my own identity was being greatly compromised.

On the night before the wedding ceremony, with considerable misgivings, I went to the *mikvah*, a ritual bath and short ceremony required of each Jewish woman before marriage. Despite my ambivalence I had decided to see the entire process through, and I asked my mother, who had come to Israel for the wedding, to accompany me. We arrived at dusk that Monday evening at a modern *mikvah* just off a main street in downtown Tel Aviv.

After greeting us in a small reception room, the female attendant led me to a private chamber, where I was instructed to bathe and wash my hair. Afterward, I was given a comb and told I must remove any knots in my hair so as not to block the purifying effects of the water. With only my mother and the attendant in the room, I walked from the bathtub across the tile floor and climbed down a ladder into a small, deep pool of water. In the shadows I repeated the blessings recited by the attendant and immersed myself, toes and fingers held apart so that the water could circulate freely. As I said the words and sprang up and down in the dark, cool water, I could hear the voices of countless other women murmuring their own blessings along with me, women who had come long before, women with whom I differed in lifestyle and belief, yet with whom I shared a heritage. Shaken by this experience, I emerged from the pool, moved and understanding in an almost transcendent way the deep power of ritual and belief.

We returned to the hotel from the *mikvah* to find messages from Alicia and Jack's sisters, who had wished to come along to the ceremony bearing traditional honey cakes. Embarrassed, I telephoned each and explained that I had not known enough about the tradition to share it with them.

On February 13, we left Israel for London on the first leg of a wedding trip that would eventually take us to the United States. That very day the Ethiopian government raised gasoline prices dramatically. Taxi drivers, students, and members of the armed forces took to the streets in fury, reacting with a protest unprecedented in its size and vehemence. Yet as surprising as were the demonstrations, more startling was the response—the government backed down, leaving the once powerless in the streets with the first inkling of their potential strength.

This first protest, and its success, led to others. A wave of marches swept the capital. By late February, the cabinet had resigned and a new prime minister was appointed. The burgeoning trouble was now beginning to be reported in the international press, where we first read about it while at my Texas home. We called our family in Ethiopia and were told that this was certainly a temporary disturbance, one that would quiet down. Despite reports of widespread disruption, business was said to be proceeding as usual. One week later, reassured by the continuing positive news, we shipped all of our wedding gifts to Addis Ababa, including a new set of English pottery in a pattern with the prophetic name Gypsy.

Along with the pottery traveled some sentimental treasures from my childhood—a porcelain pig cookie jar that had held treats for as long as I could remember, a brown stone bust of an unidentified Oriental man whom we had always affectionately called Walter, and Mrs. Victor's dishes. The dishes were a setting for twenty-four with an extraordinary array of covered serving pieces, ideal for the many dinner parties that would be at the center of our social life in the Ethiopian capital. Over fifty years old, the porcelain had been fired in Germany and painted in France. Their simple black and white border rimmed with gold was beginning to show the effects of time and loving use. But more important to me than the beauty of the porcelain was its story.

The dishes had belonged to Paula Victor, whom my parents had first met as an elderly widow teaching at our synagogue nursery school. I was one of many fortunate children who began school in her class, nurtured by her intelligence, grace, and affection. The daughter of a Jewish banker from Hamburg, Mrs. Victor had barely escaped the Holocaust with her husband and daughter. She left Germany on one of the last boats out in 1938 and managed to ship ahead some treasured possessions, including her wedding china.

In the early 1960s an increasingly frail Mrs. Victor decided to join her daughter who had settled in Israel. But she could not take with her her wedding porcelain, cumbersome to ship and, in any event, too large for her tiny retirement apartment in Haifa. She decided to give the set to a close friend, my mother, who at the time of my wedding gave it to me. A treasured reminder of a beloved teacher, years of friendship, and the vagaries of life, Mrs. Victor's well-traveled china would now have a new home in Addis Ababa.

But the promise of calm in Ethiopia was not to be. As we were about to return there in late March, the army began increasingly to assert itself and more changes were in the wind. A commission of inquiry was established to look into the disposition of public money and property. Powerful Ethiopians were now talking worriedly among themselves, trying to exorcise the fear beginning to permeate their lives. On the advice of the family in Addis Ababa, we delayed our return and spent the Passover holiday in Israel. I had planned to return to Ambober for the Beta Israel Passover, called *Fasika*. I capitulated only when it became clear that growing instability in the north and newly imposed travel restrictions would have scuttled my plans in any event.

We finally returned to Addis Ababa in April, when the protests had waned and the country appeared to have regained its equilibrium. Life in the capital slowly returned to its accustomed patterns, although there was still an undercurrent of tension. Perhaps in an attempt to quiet fears or simply to deny them, social life resumed with a vengeance.

One sunny day in early May, a crowd gathered to celebrate the independence of the state of Israel at a party thrown by one of the Adenite families to mark an additional event of local importance: the long-awaited completion of their handsome new stone and marble villa. Buffet tables were filled with Middle Eastern and Italian foodstuffs, along with the customary *injera* and *wat*. As children ran and played around the beautifully landscaped compound, with its frail, newly planted trees and shrubs, adults quietly talked over coffee about the wisdom of building so lavish a home in the current climate. Three months later the house was quietly sold at a loss, its owners returning with their possessions to one of the modern apartment buildings in the center of town.

Still in a festive mood from our wedding trip, with no further political developments to dampen our optimism, we decided to throw a party ourselves to offer friends an official welcome to our home. We invited everyone we knew, along with anyone they cared to bring, to a cocktail buffet at our apartment on Benin Sefer. Family, members of the Adenite community, Ethiopian friends, and individuals of many nationalities swept in and out of our apartment. One American couple, themselves new acquaintances just arrived for an assignment with the U.N., brought along yet newer friends of theirs. We would only later realize that the newer friends, a charming Hungarian doctor and his wife, were the first of what was to become a wave of Eastern Europeans invited to live in the capital, a subtle but tangible precursor of the coming shift away from the West.

On some occasions we did succeed in shutting out temporarily the increasingly troubled world outside. Alicia and Salamone's son, Jochanan, had his thirteenth birthday in early June, and it was decided to celebrate his *bar mitzvah* in Ethiopia. Most of the Adenite men participated in the service, along with Yosef Berhanu, the leader of the Falasha community and longtime family friend. The tiny Addis Ababa synagogue overflowed with Alicia's international array of friends: Syrians, Lebanese, French, Swedes, Armenians, and Spaniards, none of whom had ever before been to a *bar mitzvah*. As Jochanan emerged after the ceremony, the elegantly dressed women threw small, wrapped candies at him—all were later gathered up by the *zabanya* and given away to a crowd of ragged children who had gathered outside the compound.

That evening, Alicia and Salamone invited several hundred people to a festive party at the Addis Ababa Hilton. One week later the curfew was to begin, but on this night all celebrated a young boy's coming of age, dancing past midnight to Israeli folk tunes, Western popular music, and traditional Ethiopian songs played by an Ethiopian band on saxophone, guitar, and vibes. The buffet tables were crowded with continental and Ethiopian cuisine, while one table held generous platters of roasted kosher meat called *mishwi*, specially prepared for the occasion by Salamone and his cook. An earnest Ethiopian photographer crouched here and there taking hundreds of shots of the elegant crowd. Regrettably, the photographer disappeared during the turbulent weeks that followed, taking with him mementos of a last festive evening on which people had forgotten that a revolution was beginning outside their door.

My days had once again become busy as I worked on the liturgical materials gathered the prior fall, planning all the time to return north to witness and record the next cycle of Beta Israel holidays in September. My friend Abba Marqos visited frequently. Noting my struggle to transcribe the Falasha liturgy, he located a former student from the Theological College who was both expert in Ge'ez and who spoke English. A young man in his early twenties, Tamrat became my research assistant, coming to our apartment to help me transcribe the texts of the Falasha liturgy from the tapes. Together we struggled daily to decipher prayer texts that, as Father Marqos had once so amusingly remarked, "even God himself could not understand."

Then, too, the rainy season was almost upon us and our apartment was still a bare, if elegant, bachelor's abode. We set about making it a home, ordering a table for the dining room that could expand to accommodate the many friends we hoped to entertain during the rainy months ahead. The long-anticipated walnut desk, with its accompanying armchair upholstered in rose velvet, arrived late in May, and with bookshelves freshly installed along one wall, my study was suddenly complete.

Life was full of promise, and as the rains increased, we settled into the nest we had begun to build. The days resumed their leisurely pattern. I established a routine of working quietly in my study during the mornings and afternoons, broken by short walks in the garden. Occasionally I took time off to fulfill a social obligation with my sisters-in-law or to go to the university.

I had discovered that, with a bit of organization, the house virtually ran itself. By word of mouth I had located an excellent cook, an elderly Eritrean woman named Haddas who had worked over the years for both Italians and Israelis. Haddas had mastered many Italian dishes, including a creamy lasagna, a spicy minestrone, and, above all, a wonderful, thick-crusted pizza. She also knew the basics of Middle Eastern cookery, along with her native Ethiopian cuisine. Haddas spoke mainly Tigrinya but could get along with a smattering of Amharic, Italian, and Hebrew. I knew no Tigrinya, but we somehow managed to communicate in a language of our own. Inevitably, anyone within earshot would be reduced to laughter when overhearing Haddas tell me in our special pidgin that "*Salamone bet rotze eggs*," a mixture of Amharic, Hebrew, and English indicating that my brother-in-law's household needed to borrow some eggs.

Occasionally Jack and I went together to one of the markets owned and run by Greeks, stocking up on whatever imported items were available. Unaccustomed to the unreliable shipments, I at first thought Jack's purchase of multiple items of whatever he wanted excessive. I was later to learn that his tactic was also a defense against imports often spoiled by the many months in transit.

Local fruits and vegetables, in contrast, were bountiful and varied. Avocados, usually expensive in the United States, were not eaten by Ethiopians and hence were available by the kilo for pennies, along with mangos, papayas, bananas, custard apples, and melons. My brother-in-law Salamone was particularly adept at picking produce, and sometimes I would accompany him, listening to his many entertaining stories about his father and their early years in Ethiopia. We all lived mainly off the local economy, receiving milk and homemade cheese from a small concern run by an elderly Italian woman and buying bread and pastries from a nearby Italian bakery. We drank strong, dark Ethiopian coffee, blended and ground at a store just around the corner, at the bottom of Benin Sefer. A notable exception was the collection of European wines Jack kept in the pantry, which he restocked whenever a shipment arrived at the liquor store in the piazza.

As often as we could, Jack and I spent the evening alone at home, sending Haddas off to rest while we prepared a light evening meal together. It was mainly Jack who cooked, while I sat on a stool in the corner of our large yellow kitchen, sipping a glass of wine, sometimes preparing vegetables for a salad. We traded tales of our vastly different childhoods—my conventional, stable American background contrasted with his international, turbulent life. When he was fourteen, Jack, along with Moshe and Danny, was sent to boarding school in England. He did not return to Addis Ababa for a decade, but was in the end persuaded by his father to give up his studies and join the family business.

We slowly began to invite friends to our home, starting with a series of Sunday brunches featuring homemade waffles and pancakes. We would host a mixture of Ethiopian friends and whomever happened to be in town and in need of a warm welcome. We began to become more involved with members of the diplomatic community and enjoyed the stimulating company of people from all over the world.

The Shelemay family had long been at the center of an international network. In addition to the numerous friends and business acquaintances who came to Addis Ababa and were graciously received, there came by mail many odd inquiries for which the postal authorities deemed the Shelemays the appropriate recipients. The family decided that I should take over the task of answering these letters, since the great majority were from inquisitive Americans. These letters, variously addressed to "The Addis Ababa Synagogue" or to "The Jewish Community of Ethiopia," ranged from general inquiries about the country to very specific (and often inappropriate) requests for statistics—one requested information about the number of Jewish mayors and congressmen in Ethiopia. Some letters sought information about the Falasha, which I either answered myself or passed on to Yosef Berhanu during our frequent visits. Often, foreign visitors simply dropped by the Shelemay offices while they were in town, asking about the synagogue on the compound or the community. Many times I would smile as I greeted a visitor for coffee or dinner, remembering my own first encounter with Jack: at the time I too had appeared to be one more curious American tourist landing on the Shelemay doorstep.

Within this active social network, I slowly began to be aware of the many close relationships that the Shelemays had with Ethiopians. While they were always aware of their status as foreigners, the Shelemays had built strong attachments to the country and its people. This network did not generally include my sisters-in-law, who had few Ethiopian friends and who socialized mainly with Adenite women or with the wives of diplomats on long-term assignments. The wives of Jack's brothers were Israelis who had come to Ethiopia as newlyweds. They had little in common with the Ethopian women who, even in the capital, led sheltered lives apart from the public worlds of their husbands. The few Ethiopian women who had been educated abroad and had returned home occupied what could only be described as a social limbo on the periphery of Ethiopian society. No longer candidates to become the proper, traditional wives that even highly educated Ethiopian males usually desired, they pursued modest careers, mostly living with extended families or, rarely, alone in their own apartments. They had even less in common with the women of the permanent foreign community than did their more traditional counterparts.

It was different for the Shelemay men, who had close Ethiopian friends from years of residency in the country. Jack had Ethiopian intimates from his years at the Haile Selassie I University and his active participation in the Round Table, an all-male club involved in civic and philanthropic affairs. On many afternoons, after work, Ethiopian friends would drop by for drinks. These were convivial gatherings at which the Shelemay wives were welcome, though few visitors ever brought their own wives along. Not surprisingly, our visitors were mainly members of the Ethiopian aristocracy or the growing middle class.

The most frequent visitor was a high officer of the Ethiopian army who was descended from an aristocratic family and had been educated abroad. He often came to Salamone's apartment to visit and to share information. A tall, commanding figure, as befitted his rank, General Habte one day arrived with invitations for all the Shelemay family to attend the wedding reception for his daughter Abebetch. Thus, in mid-June 1974, I attended my first Ethiopian wedding party.

As we entered the Addis Ababa Hilton and stood in the long hallway that led into the main ballroom, we could see the fresh carcasses of beef, still twitching from the slaughter, hanging from metal racks. From these would be cut pieces of *tere sega*, raw meat, considered to be a great delicacy. We entered the festive ballroom, where elegant men in tuxedos and and women in formal gowns were already seated, platters filled with *tere sega* in the center of each table.

As we began to circulate within the crowd of government officials, members of the aristocracy, diplomats, and permanent residents, we slowly began to sense an extraordinary tension lurking below the seemingly jovial surface. Each guest greeted the others cautiously, skirting past this one, avoiding the gaze of the other. Cabinet members well known to be close friends sat on opposite sides of the room, glancing at each other and quickly looking away, unsure of how to act. Orchestra Ethiopia, a small ensemble of musicians drawn from all corners of the empire and brought to the capital under the sponsorship of the emperor, played all the while, performing Ethiopian songs whose double meanings now seemed more ominous than usual.

Rumor had it that the commission of inquiry appointed in late March would soon be announcing its first round of findings. Fear was rampant. Individuals worried that they would be accused of graft or other crimes against the state. At the wedding party all these terrors seemed to well up, smothering the usual warmth and interaction.

Barely a few days later events began to hurtle out of control. Late in June, a new coordinating committee of the armed forces was established; shortly thereafter a number of former officials were asked to turn themselves in for further investigation. In this manner, General Habte and virtually all the notables of the old order voluntarily packed their bags and were delivered by their drivers to what became a most feared prison in the bowels of the Menelik Palace.

7

TRANSITIONS

One evening in late June 1974, we arrived at a diplomat's home for an 8:00 P.M. dinner. Just as we began what promised to be a leisurely cocktail hour, the host received an emergency telephone call from his country's embassy—a curfew had been declared, effective at 9:00 P.M. that evening. Hurriedly, the cook placed portions of the uneaten dinner on paper plates, wrapped each in tin foil, and handed them to the guests as we rushed out the door.

Thus began the curfews that were to regulate our lives in the months to come. The lively nightlife of the capital virtually ground to a halt, in large part because the hours of the curfew often shifted. During periods of tension, on days when particularly important announcements were made, the curfews stretched from 7:30 P.M. to 6:00 A.M., while during calmer spells the curfew was midnight to 6:00 A.M. Of greatest concern were the frequent changes, which left everyone nervous that they might be caught unaware. Several unfortunate individuals still on the streets after curfew were wounded or killed by soldiers who impulsively shot at their speeding cars. Although physicians and officials involved with critical services such as telecommunications received special permits that could be used in an emergency, few were willing to risk an encounter with a soldier or army unit who might not notice their permit or might not stop to ask questions before firing.

By mid-July it had become increasingly frustrating to conduct business, particularly international commerce that required the cooperation and approval of bank officials and government agencies entrusted with export procedures. After several months of deliberations, the dreaded commission of inquiry had taken action against a number of high-ranking former officials, accusing them of "abuse and malfeasance." The charges left those still in positions of authority increasingly unsure of how their daily actions would be judged. As a result, most were reluctant to make any decisions at all, reducing a routine if cumbersome export process to chaos.

The emperor receded farther into the background, isolated from the world around him, living under virtual house arrest in the Jubilee Palace as the Armed Forces Coordinating Committee widened its purview. The committee slowly took charge of all military and police forces, declaring an amnesty for former prisoners of the emperor and inviting political refugees from his regime to return home. At the same time, it issued a series of proclamations that promised to reshape Ethiopia's future.

On July 8, 1974, the ever more powerful coordinating committee, now calling itself the Derg, moved aggressively, declaring a thirteen-point program titled "Ethiopia Tikdem," a motto meaning "Ethiopia forward." In its initial formulation, the platform of Ethiopia Tikdem pledged loyalty to and support for the crown, while seeking to offer reassurance to those apprehensive after the first wave of arrests. The program also pledged a revised constitution with attention to greater equality for all. It admitted that a famine had swept the north and that international aid was needed to help alleviate the suffering. Declaring that these reforms would be achieved without bloodshed, Ethiopia Tikdem was a document of energy and optimism. After months of vacillation a new direction had been set, one that to the eyes of most held great promise.

Despite its pledge of loyalty to the monarchy, the Derg's commitment to the emperor remained in question. Through the month of August and into early September, the Derg slowly took away all aspects of the crown's power and resources, transferring them to other government agencies or to its own direct control. One by one, the formerly powerful Crown Council and the Imperial Review Court, or Chillot, the final court of appeals for all disputes, were disbanded. Ownership of the national Ambassa Bus Company, the St. George Brewery, and the Haile Selassie Prize Trust, as well as a number of other institutions, was transferred from imperial control to the Ministry of Finance and other agencies.

In perhaps the most stunning symbolic move, the Jubilee Palace was renamed the National Palace and the emperor was whisked away to an unspecified place for so-called protective custody, ostensibly to shield him from what was termed "the anger of his people." On September 11 Ethiopian television presented, with great fanfare, a heretofore banned documentary film called *The Hidden Hunger* by British journalist Jonathan Dimbleby, which set forth in scathing terms the emperor's neglect of the 1972 famine. At the same time, it also aired clips of the emperor's past lavish entertainments. With the final preparations completed, and with sentiment against His Imperial Majesty running high, the emperor was deposed on September 12, 1974. The Provisional Military Administrative Council (PMAC) assumed the function of the head of state, and the Ethiopian revolution officially began.

Life had gone on pretty much as usual during the months of what Blair Thomson of the BBC later called the "creeping coup." I continued to work on my dissertation, with the assistance of Tamrat. The apartment on Benin Sefer, my first real home of my own, had become a source of great pleasure, growing more comfortable with each change we made. Every Friday our gardener brought in pails of fresh flowers—lilies, roses, snapdragons— which I arranged in vases and placed all over the house. Through friends, I had met several Ethiopian painters whose works now hung in several rooms. One of my favorites was a surrealistic oil painting of a long-fingered King David plucking the ten-stringed lyre associated with Ethiopian royalty. Another was a woodcut showing a musician playing the *krar*, singing (or I so imagined) a tender rendition of *tezzeta* to the woman sitting before him.

Our large Danish dining room was now complete and, when curfews permitted, we invited friends over to sample Haddas's good cooking. Occasionally we went out to see films, sometimes at the small public theater adjoining the Municipality Building, at other times in the homes of diplomats who occasionally screened recent releases obtained through their embassies. Often, I'd take a break from my work and walk across the street to the office. Jack would send for coffee and tell me about the new difficulties he was encountering in what had always been a straightforward export process. When the sky cleared between the heavy rains and the sun came out, I'd quickly slip out to the garden where I could walk undisturbed among the rose bushes and fuchsia.

For three weeks during late July and early August, Jack went on a business trip to London and I remained at home. For a brief time, the apartment on Benin Sefer was mine alone.

My sister-in-law Alicia was away in Israel for the months of the rains, but Moshe's wife, Yona, had finally returned to Ethiopia in May with her infant daughter, Limor, whom I enjoyed greatly. Yona was a dark, somber woman in her mid-thirties. Born in Aden and raised in Israel, she had married Moshe nine years earlier. I had heard that, upon her arrival in Ethiopia, she had been so appalled by the prospect of living with the entire family at Villa Populare that she had insisted upon going to a hotel until an apartment was completed for her and Moshe on Benin Sefer. Never close to her in-laws, she lived in a world of her own with a network of her own friends. Yona and I spent many hours together, taking French lessons from a woman who drilled us with nonsensical vocabulary cards and making plans to begin tennis lessons as soon as the rains abated.

Good company, too, was Jack's sister Aviva, who had returned to Ethiopia before the rains. Petite and beautiful, she lived in her small gem of an apartment, working in the office each day and managing aspects of the Shelemay real estate holdings. Aviva had gone to the Addis Ababa British School and had later attended high school in Israel. Afterward, she had lived for a time in England, studying gemology and working in the travel industry. Like a small bird seeking a comfortable nest, she migrated between London, Addis Ababa, and Tel Aviv, no single place being capable of satisfying all her needs. She is a woman of many cultures, at home in none.

Slowly, I came to be more comfortable with my new way of life and with the expectations of the community in which I lived. Everyone knew that I was doing research on Ethiopian music and that I spent most of my time in my study writing. My sisters-in-law learned to respect my work hours, and I, in turn, spent time with them while avoiding the regular round of teas and daytime social activities. I was treated graciously by all, the force of the Shelemay name ensuring my acceptance despite my refusal to take on a conventional woman's role in this strange sort of suburbia.

Throughout the rainy season, we continued to follow our daily routines, watching political events unfold around us. No one was saddened to see the emperor deposed, since he was widely perceived as having lost his ability to govern the country effectively, as the neglect of the Wollo famine had so tragically demonstrated. The program announced by the PMAC in July was to all evidence benign, and the future appeared to hold positive changes for the country.

We had been surprised that Haile Selassie's removal from power had not elicited more response from the peasantry. For all their lives, they had viewed the man as a near deity with absolute power, murmuring his name in their prayers each week at church and as a sacred oath. Yet his removal had not prompted a ground swell of support from the countryside. In the capital there was euphoria as he was escorted out of the palace and into oblivion, events to be followed, however, by new and escalating conflicts among the PMAC and various urban factions.

The Jewish fall holidays were once again upon us. I had, until the last minute, hoped to return to Gondar, but the developments of September 12 rendered any travel north out of the question. Enormously disappointed, I threw myself into preparations for our own celebrations in Addis Ababa. Alicia and Salamone were still in Israel, and the responsibility for any family plans had fallen to Jack and me. In a burst of enthusiasm we decided to invite a large group of friends to lunch on Rosh Hashanah, the Jewish New Year.

After the morning synagogue service, a crowd congregated at our house. Moshe, Yona, Aviva, and Danny were invited, along with the Banins, Aharonnees, and their four adult children. Two Jewish American researchers joined us, as did the families of several other Adenite clans. We set extra tables throughout the dining area of our apartment, altogether laying places for twenty-seven. The tables were covered with damask cloths from Syria, embroidered in gold and silver thread, brought to Addis Ababa by one of Alicia's friends. Roses from the garden were arranged at the center of each table and in vases throughout the house. Moshe's and Salamone's cooks joined Haddas in the preparations, ensuring a variety of offerings for the festive meal. Mrs. Victor's china graced the table for the first and last holiday in our home, with all its serving pieces brought forth to hold roast meat, fasolia, salads, and vegetables. For a few hours we toasted the holiday, eating pomegranates, dates, and apples dipped in honey, expressing more fervently than usual our hopes for a good year ahead.

It would not be a quiet new year. Within the month, a series of new regulations began slowly to transform urban life. In early October, the import of all luxury items was banned. The municipal councils that had run the local governments were abolished, their structures dismembered, with nothing to take their place.

The most controversial move was the announcement on October 17 of Zemetcha, the Campaign for Development through Cooperation. Under this program, urban Ethiopian youth would be sent to rural areas to explain the political changes to the peasantry and to institute programs of aid. From its inception, Zemetcha was controversial. Some families, especially concerned at the prospect of young girls being sent unsupervised into the countryside, sent their children into hiding rather than comply with the order.

Privately, many speculated that Zemetcha was designed less to help the rural poor than to rid the city of its most consistently radical element, the students. Since the 1960s the students had often protested the inequities of the emperor's regime, and there was little doubt that their activism, which had contributed to the success of the revolution, might well prove as difficult for the new government to contain as it had for the old.

It also became clear that some Zemetcha assignments were punitive or simply humiliating. We began to see groups of workers in green Zemetcha uniforms doing manual labor around the city. One day I called Father Marqos, who for several weeks had declined my repeated invitations to come over for lunch or tea. Only when I pressed for an explanation did he blurt out, "I've been taken to Zemetcha." Days later, he finally agreed to see me, embarrassed that he was forced to wear the Zemetcha uniform and cap instead of clerical garb and to sweep the streets of Addis Ababa.

Around that time, I left Ethiopia for a visit to the United States. I had been isolated for too long; I needed to consult my advisors at Michigan and to visit my family. My research assistant, Tamrat, was leaving for Zemetcha, and his departure disrupted our progress in transcribing the Falasha liturgy. The rainy season, never a lively time for foreign researchers, had been unusually quiet, with few visiting scholars around and available for conversation. My efforts to contact Ethiopian colleagues had proved frustrating for months—most were preoccupied with the political situation. I had not seen as much as usual of my friend Tesemma, who was now, like so many others, being sent to the countryside.

With so much of the faculty away, the university had suspended day classes, while expatriate professors maintained some evening courses. In mid-October, special courts were established to try former officials charged with corruption and maladministration. Individuals were accused of having neglected their duties and of having allowed the Wollo famine to rage unabated. News clips of the dead and dying, no longer banned, were broadcast each day on Ethiopian television and became the central rallying point for the revolution. I was glad to get away, hoping to be able push the tension aside for even a short time.

But I encountered news of the trials everywhere I traveled in the United States, and I began to have nightmares about Ethiopia. On November 23, 1974, I dreamed that I received a telephone call from Ababetch, the daughter of General Habte, who was still in custody at the Menelik Palace. "Father has been shot," she screamed. I awoke shaking, thankful it was only a dream.

Later that afternoon I heard a newscast announcing that Aman Andom, head of the PMAC, had been deposed and, along with two former prime ministers, sixty former officials, and uncounted members of the armed forces, summarily executed. Many of those who had willingly turned themselves in to custody barely six months earlier had been murdered. Shaken by the news, I left the next day for Ethiopia, too worried to be away any longer. I arrived to find that General Habte had somehow escaped execution, although he remained in prison under conditions described as increasingly brutal. The deaths marked a tragic transition, however, to the point where this revolution of peace and promise, or at least this illusion of such, betrayed itself.

At the end of November, a series of explosions rocked the capital. Benin Sefer shook from a bomb hidden in the movie theater we so often attended, next to the Municipality Building. A second explosive device went off at the Wabe Shebelle Hotel. These were the first indications of armed resistance to the heretofore unobstructed actions of the military. In response, the Derg posted tanks and guards with machine guns throughout the capital. Addis Ababa became an armed camp. For some weeks, jeeps loaded with recruits carrying automatic weapons patrolled the streets, guns sometimes firing accidentally as their vehicles hit bumps in the rough roads.

The Derg began to publicize the former regime's use of national resources, including stories that the emperor had secreted a huge sum of money and gold ingots in Swiss banks. The mention of stolen billions aroused great anger among workers and peasants with an annual per capita income of less than a hundred Ethiopian dollars.

In the city, individuals struggled to understand the dimensions of the emperor's rumored hoard. One day, Jack's secretary of many years walked in and asked Jack if he thought such stories were believable. Jack told her no, he didn't think the emperor could have hidden so much, the sum was too astronomical. "How many zeros are there in a billion?" asked Mulunesh, still trying to grasp the figures. "More than you can count," answered Jack, increasingly uncomfortable with the entire exchange.

Everyone had begun to be extremely circumspect about what they said concerning current events. Both the mail and the telephones were said to be monitored by the government. Hearsay had been used as evidence against a number of individuals on trial, and since the identities of the members of the Derg were a closely held secret, no one could be certain through which networks a comment might travel. Mulunesh was married to an army officer who, despite his relatively low rank, might present a threat.

The November executions and countercoup had obviously masked political and philosophical disagreements within the Derg itself. By late November, the leadership had changed direction and on December 20 declared Ethiopia a socialist state.

Socialism was an unfamiliar word to most Ethiopians. There was no real equivalent in Amharic and no new term was offered by the revolutionary council. Instead, most of the council simply used the English word, explaining in a declaration that it meant all resources would eventually be brought under governmental control for the common good. Further guidelines were issued for cultural development and for equality among the various ethnic groups, building upon the tenets of Ethiopia Tikdem. Plans were announced for self-administration and popular participation in local councils, called *kebele*.

In the area of foreign affairs, the Derg called for noninterference, presaging an end to decades of close relations with the West and opening the door to a series of new alignments. In the preceding weeks, I had on several occasions encountered a large number of Chinese in the piazza. Now it was announced that they had come to aid with rural development.

In late December, a series of large demonstrations was organized to show public support for the new socialist policies. Thousands marched through the capital, holding aloft banners that read "Let the Ethiopian People Be Victorious!" and "The Ethiopian People Will Manage On Their Own!" We watched from the roof of our building as tanks, soldiers, and milling thousands made their way through the streets of the piazza.

Almost immediately, religious life throughout the country was affected. During the period of the creeping coup, religious freedom had been a pressing issue, especially among Muslims and other minorities. The previous April, mass demonstrations had been mounted against the church. A particularly volatile issue was the excessive number of Orthodox Christian holidays, including some 180 obligatory fast days when only one meal with animal products could be consumed, a practice that disrupted agriculture. Finally, on December 23, the government reduced the total number of official religious holidays to twelve, four each for Muslims, Orthodox Christians, and Protestants. Even as the Derg attacked the church, declaring that all Ethiopians must adopt nationalism and patriotism as their own personal faith, at the same time it pledged to preserve the "world-renowned cultural artifacts" of the country. These most certainly included the churches and monasteries that contained some of Ethiopia's greatest treasures.

Other attempts to redress the long-standing inequalities affecting ethnic and religious minorities continued in the following days with measures such as the institution of radio broadcasts in Oromo, the language known colloquially as Galla and used collectively by all Oromo-speaking tribes. These new policies in fact marked the end of the long domination of Ethiopian political and cultural life by the Christian Amharas. For centuries, the hegemony of this powerful people, who comprised less than 40 percent of the Ethiopian population, had been maintained by the monarchy and the church. High on the Derg's agenda was a desire to eliminate Christian Amhara power and, along with it, any threat from former leadership, while equalizing the conditions for other ethnic and religious minorities. In particular, the

Beta Israel stood to gain from these new revolutionary policies, which would give them an equal status they had never known.

To achieve these goals, the Derg first would have to address economic issues, which they began to do on January 1, 1975, by nationalizing the three commercial banks and all insurance companies. In fact, the largest bank, the Commercial Bank of Ethiopia, was already owned by the government, and the Addis Ababa Bank had been a public share company. The action primarily served to take over the Banco di Roma, a branch of an Italian banking enterprise, and to replace the existing management with a new one. At the same time, the government pledged compensation for both Ethiopian and foreign investors.

It seemed clear that other nationalizations would follow. Most people agreed that the factories were likely to be the next target if the government continued on its current course. So far most of the permanent foreign community had escaped the direct effects of the new policies, but it now became clear that those with large businesses were potentially threatened. The Shelemays, with some of the largest holdings, had the most to lose.

After he had first settled in Ethiopia, following the debacle in Aden, Shalom Shelemay had begun to import textiles from Europe and the Far East to a receptive Ethiopian market. Over the years, he and his sons had expanded the family business to include the export of diverse commodities including coffee, hides and skins, oilseeds, grains, beans, and civet, a substance used in the perfume and cosmetic industry. At the same time they had moved into real estate, constructing the two buildings on Benin Sefer, and into textile manufacture.

In 1972 the Shelemays built Ethiopian Pickling and Tanning to process raw skins into semifinished leather, in partnership with overseas investors. Having long shipped raw hides and skins abroad, they viewed this as a logical step in the development of the Ethiopian leather industry. Their factory was located on a tract of land on the outskirts of the city, on a hillside at the bottom of which ran a small stream, an offshoot of the Awash River. The construction of the factory had in fact been greeted with a court case brought by a commercial florist in the adjacent valley who was concerned that the factory would disturb the wedding parties that frequently rented his gardens. It was eventually the emperor's decision that the plant should be built on the land the Shelemay's had bought for that purpose, the emperor supporting economic development over possible aesthetic considerations. The aesthetic issue was soon largely put to rest, however, when Salamone planted a flower garden along the hillside running from the plant down to the river. By the fall of 1974, the garden was filled with snapdragons, lilies, and roses, each growing in neat rows amid the eucalyptus and pine trees.

The factory was a large building constructed of cement blocks with a corrugated tin roof. The tanning operation processed raw sheep and goat skins, delivered from the countyside where they had been wet-salted after slaughter. The skins were soaked and processed in huge rotating drums filled with chemicals and then packed wet, in heavy plastic bags, for export to Europe and the Far East. Several shifts worked to fill orders, sometimes around the clock when the supply of fresh skins was abundant, such as the days after important Ethiopian holidays that called for the slaughter of livestock for feasting.

There had already been intimations of the nationalizations to come. During the Ethiopian Christmas season in early January, the PMAC had decreed that all hides and skins coming from either slaughterhouses or individuals must be donated to the famine relief commission where they could then be sold to merchants and tanneries at a profit. One day the Shelemay men were called by an official of the relief commission, who told them to meet him at a designated place and to bring along their checkbook.

An hour later, they arrived at a compound in the city that was filled with mounds of freshly slaughtered hides and skins. They were shown to one large pile and were told that these skins now belonged to them. They were to write a check then and there to be used for famine relief. Left with no choice in the matter, Jack wrote the check and the skins were brought to the factory for finishing.

On February 4, the morning of our first wedding anniversary, Jack and I awoke to hear on the radio that large concerns, including Ethiopian Pickling and Tanning, had been transferred to government control late the previous day. Jack and his brothers went to the office, where at first everything appeared as usual. But later that day, when a check that Jack had signed on behalf of the tanning company was returned unpaid by the bank, which had declared his signature no longer valid, the full impact of the announcement hit us. The next day a government official called to say that he would be coming to take an inventory and to effect the formal takeover. On February 5, in a subdued atmosphere, two officials came and with the help of Salamone, Jack, Moshe, and Danny took control of the factory.

In addition to the nationalizations, other concerns preoccupied us on February 4. For several weeks, there had been increasingly frightening news from Asmara, where fighting had again flared up since the execution of Lieutenant General Aman Andom, former head of the Derg. General Aman, an Eritrean, had visited the northern province during his brief tenure as head of the PMAC, and for the first time in the long struggle for Eritrean independence from Ethiopian control there seemed to be the possibility for a negotiated settlement. But after the November murders and Aman's bloody death, any hope of accommodation evaporated as a vicious battle erupted for Asmara itself.

The second oldest Shelemay son, Ben, lived in Asmara with his family. There he managed a large textile factory in which the Shelemays were minor partners, also serving as agents to distribute the goods to the local market. Ben, his wife, Ruth, and their two young sons lived in a modern villa in the city. As the fighting had spread during the previous days, we had received a series of disturbing telephone calls from Ben's family, who reported being unable to leave the house, the sounds of gunshots and mortar fire raging throughout their neighborhood. Now the electricity was out and evacuation appeared imminent.

In mid-morning of February 4 we received word that all foreigners were being evacuated from Asmara by their respective embassies. With Jack and his brothers at the office trying to assess the impact of the nationalizations, Yona, Aviva, and I went to the Addis Ababa Hilton, the central arrival point for all evacuees. People milled about in confusion as representatives of various embassies tried to arrange accommodations for hundreds of disoriented people. The coffee shop was overflowing with friends and relatives waiting for word of each planeload of arrivals, evacuees who would then be bused to the Hilton for placement. News teams, barred from Asmara because of the heavy fighting, camped out alongside the hotel parking lot, hoping to get information from the north and photograph tearful reunions.

In the late afternoon, Ruth and her boys arrived, haggard and shaken from the harrowing experience; Ben had remained in Asmara. We took them home, along with several other friends and relatives from Asmara, absorbing them among the various family and friends living on Benin Sefer.

The nationalizations and evacuations of February 4 left us depleted and depressed, our first wedding anniversary forgotten amid the mounting problems. Since the executions of November 23 and the declaration of Ethiopian socialism, we had suspected that we were witnessing a policy change that would ultimately threaten our future. But there had remained the possibility of a reprieve, a chance that the process would somehow stop, or that the revolution would change its course. With the nationalization of the factories, the most optimistic among us could no longer view the revolution with enthusiasm, nor could the most cynical brush it off as a passing disruption. Although we did not discuss the future in great detail, and usually greeted pessimistic comments with an angry response, at heart everyone knew that things would never be the same.

Lives do not disintegrate in an instant, though the dramatic moments have their impact and exact their toll. Rather, each day brings new, small realizations, and with them new fears. By early January I had begun to find it difficult to concentrate on my work. I'd leave my desk and wander around the house, thoughts, even hopes, of evacuation filling my mind.

I began to play a game with myself, over and over again. If I were to be evacuated with only an hour's notice and could take only ten things with me, what would they be? I'd spend hours making imaginary lists, striking one choice and adding another. What if I could take twenty items, or only five?

Although our personal possessions were nothing in comparison to the lives and issues at stake, I was obsessed with the fear that we might lose all that we owned in the burgeoning crisis. Perhaps because my own work was the only aspect of our lives and future over which I had some control, I was particularly frantic that it would be lost. In early January I began to send things out of the country. I first mailed valuable books, tapes, and research materials to Texas, gratefully accepting the offers of friends at various embassies to send these irreplaceable materials out of the country for me. Later that month, when a friend completed his job contract in Addis Ababa and returned to England, he took with him our most valuable and sentimental items for safekeeping at Jack's sister's home in London. In late January I transferred Mrs. Victor's dishes to the home of friends in the diplomatic corps who offered to store them for us, knowing that their possessions would almost certainly be packed and shipped afterward if they were suddenly evacuated. In order not to arouse suspicion, I quietly took the entire set of porcelain out of the house myself, carrying one or two carefully wrapped pieces at a time, whenever I went to the office or the garden. Once the entire set was in the trunk of Jack's car, we drove one evening to our friends' villa and unloaded the dishes.

Everyone was in a dark mood. Although the import-export business had not been nationalized in early February, along with Ethiopian Pickling, trade had ground to a virtual halt, so great was the uncertainty about what would happen next. Immediately after the nationalizations, we found an intrepid mover who, for a substantial sum, managed to slip into Benin Sefer, pack small items of our household, and send them out of the country. Mrs. Victor's dishes were picked up quietly from our friends' home and spent the next several years stored in a Tel Aviv warehouse. Suddenly, our apartment was quite bare, returned to the way I had found it a year and a half earlier.

Things steadily worsened, with a state of emergency declared in Eritrea on February 15 and massive protests in Addis Ababa against the violence. The series of revolutionary proclamations continued, some symbolic, others substantive. In a move that might, in better days, have caused considerable amusement, the Solomonic lion was deposed. Even ships were rechristened: the Ethiopian Shipping Corporation's *Lion of Judah* became overnight the *Lion of Ethiopia*.

In early March, in one of its most far-reaching proclamations, the PMAC declared all rural land nationalized. For centuries, much of highland Ethiopia had been owned by members of the aristocracy and by the Ethiopian church. Much of the rural population had been tenant farmers, paying taxes or a portion of their crops in exchange for use of the land. Others had received land from the church or from various princes, property that was then passed down from generation to generation in an elaborate system of land tenure. No problem engaged the rural population as actively as the debate over land rights and land ownership, and it was common for an individual to spend a great amount of time engaged in litigation. Now the system of land ownership long at the basis of the social and economic structure of Ethiopia was officially dissolved.

Ethiopians and expatriates alike were affected by these nationalizations, many dramatically so. Overnight the supporting economic base of the Ethiopian church disappeared, the enormous income from tenant farmers on its former lands gone. With these lands, too, went much of the incentive to join the church, for members of the clergy had customarily received small tracts that would remain in their families in reward for their service.

Although formerly landless peasants were now entitled to own land, and long-disfranchised groups like the Beta Israel stood to gain from the decree, the process of actually redistributing land proved to be chaotic. Men who had formerly litigated for familial lands were now willing to fight for them, and a wave of violence swept the northern provinces. The transition in southern locales went more smoothly, with Zemetcha workers sent to aid the process.

Most expatriates lived in urban areas and were not affected by the nationalization of farmland. Some, however, lost everything they had built up during their years in the country; among these were the Sandford family.

Brigadier Sandford had served with the British army in Ethiopia during World War II. He distinguished himself in service to the Ethiopian State and was rewarded by the emperor with a tract of land some fifteen miles north of Addis Ababa. The land overlooked a chasm of unsurpassed beauty, with a waterfall plunging from an upper cliff down to a stream below. Accepting the gift, Sandford stayed on in Ethiopia after the war and his property became known as Mulu Farm.

Always called "The Brigadier," Sandford was a slightly stooped figure with a white mustache and tortoise-rim glasses, inevitably dressed in a tweed jacket, corduroy pants, and a rumpled fedora hat, giving him the appearance of a country squire. He occupied himself with overseeing the farm, which produced milk at its dairy and boasted the first strawberries and plums in Ethiopia.

The Sandford family joined The Brigadier shortly after the war and soon became deeply involved in life in the capital. Mrs. Sandford served as director of the British Council School in Addis Ababa. When the school outgrew its early facilities, the Sandford family helped raise money to purchase a new site, a former hotel and amusement park constructed during the Italian occupation. In gratitude, the school was informally known as the Sandford School. Its enrollment included a healthy mixture of Ethiopian and foreign children, all of whom were required to participate in a daily Anglican service that Mrs. Sandford always conducted herself, with rousing renditions of "Onward Christian Soldiers" on the piano. Her eldest daughter, Eleanor, helped direct Christmas pageants and occasional productions of Gilbert and Sullivan, while the younger daughter, Pippa, with chestnut hair pulled back in a long braid, conducted the chorus.

The Brigadier died some years before the revolution. Mrs. Sandford, her daughters, and son stayed on, only to lose Mulu Farm in 1975. Shortly thereafter Mrs. Sandford died; only her son, Stephen, remained in Ethiopia. The Shelemays did not own rural land and were not immediately affected by the land nationalization. As exporters of Ethiopian crops, however, they had contracts with a number of farmers. Because of this they found themselves embroiled in a serious dispute.

The Shelemay Company had for a number of years purchased crops of haricot beans from an Italian farmer who owned land north of Addis Ababa. During the early days of the revolution, the Shelemays entered into a contract with the owner of the farm to purchase his current crop. As usual, they arranged for the farmer to send the crop, cleaned and packed in jute bags, to the seaport of Assab, from where it would be shipped abroad. When the Shelemay export brokers received the goods, payment would be made directly to the owner or, from time to time, to third parties the owner designated.

A day or two after the edict nationalizing rural land, the Shelemay office was visited by an Ethiopian gentleman bearing a letter from the farm owner stating that he should be paid a certain sum of money. But since the farm now belonged to the Ethiopian government, the Shelemays could not pay him—the individual who had signed the letter no longer owned the farm. The man kept returning to the Shelemay office, insisting that he be paid, each time becoming more agitated and demanding. Equally adamant in their refusal, the Shelemays informed the man that he could only be paid if he had a letter of authorization from the new owners, the Ethiopian government.

A few days later, the Shelemays received a telephone call from a captain who identified himself as being affiliated with the office investigating grievances by the people. He wished to see Salamone and Jack immediately. Arriving at an office that had once housed a prime minister, Jack and Salamone were met by the captain's assistant, who demanded that they make a statement.

Afterward, they were taken into the office of the captain, along-side whom sat the Ethiopian man who had demanded payment. They were greeted with a harangue:

"The time has come to quit this exploitation and the abuses of the oppressed masses. It is time to stop this imperialistic attitude. You must pay this poor man his money immediately," the captain demanded.

"But we cannot pay him without a letter of authorization from the appropriate government office," responded Salamone.

"I don't care about a letter of authorization," answered the captain, his voice rising. "Return this afternoon with a check for the full amount or you will be sent to prison."

Shaken by the threat, Jack and Salamone returned to the office and made phone calls to several government offices inquiring about the effect of making such a payment to an individual. No payment should be made, they were told, and if they did, they would be entirely responsible to the government for the same sum of money. Meanwhile, the captain called again, this time instructing them to bring cash.

Finally, Jack succeeded in reaching the official in charge of nationalized rural land and told him what had happened. "I'll take care of the matter," he replied. "In any event, don't pay cash."

Later that afternoon, Salamone and Jack went to meet the captain as previously arranged. When they told him they did not have cash, he became livid and shouted that he would send them to jail. Just then the telephone rang and the captain answered it. As he began talking in a very subdued tone of voice, Salamone and Jack realized that the call was about them. Putting down the phone, the captain turned to them and smiled.

"Well, you understand these are difficult times and we must seem to respond to the grievances of the people," he said. "You can go home."

Some days later Salamone and Jack learned that the individual bearing the letter of assignment was a relative of the captain, who had thought that, under the circumstances, he might be able to get away with extortion.

The wave of nationalizations and the resulting climate of fear thus affected everyone. Many decided to leave, those who could obtain exit visas doing so legally. But to receive an exit visa was not an easy matter, since both bank and tax clearances were required of anyone who had worked in Ethiopia. With the banks newly nationalized, and tax clearances practically impossible to obtain with so much of industry now under government control, many Ethiopians and expatriates alike began to flee the country. Ethiopians who could disguise themselves as villagers often slipped out of the capital and made their way to one of the border towns. No route was safe, however, given the war in the north, skirmishes along the southern border with Somalia, and instability in the southwest adjoining the Sudan.

Wealthy Ethiopians and some foreigners used considerable ingenuity to leave the country, some simply disappearing mysteriously overnight and never being heard from again. So many successfully escaped in chartered planes that eventually all private aircraft companies and light airplanes were nationalized.

I often fantasized about leaving, wondering how long it would take to extricate ourselves from the nationalizations past and those likely in the future. The government promised compensation for all assets, a carrot held just out of reach, suggesting that it might be profitable to remain. At home, we began to talk quietly about a future outside of Ethiopia, among family and very close friends. Each Friday evening, around Salamone's dinner table, we discussed where we might settle. One week it was Toronto, the next London, then New York. Sometimes we laughed about it, Alicia joking that we would begin our own kibbutz in Australia.

One day, I noticed that several boxes of cotton fabrics swatches from the recently nationalized Asmara textile factory were still sitting in a corner of the Shelemay office. I had for some months considered taking up a craft to help calm my nerves. I had always loved quilts, especially the one that my paternal grandmother had made by hand for my wedding. Constructed from scraps of materials she had once used to sew my childhood dresses, it was now safely stored in London with some of our other possessions.

Excited, I claimed the leftover fabrics and had them taken to our apartment. I bought a small book with simple instructions on quilting at one of the local bookstores and started to work. It looked so easy, to lay out a design and then cut the scraps and sew them together. But the few squares I painstakingly constructed turned out to be asymmetrical and uneven. Eventually I gave up in frustration, packing the materials away, to be assembled sometime, somewhere, along with the rest of our lives.

In early March 1975, Aviva, Alicia, and her children left for Israel. Life was stressful and the teenaged Jochanan was becoming increasingly isolated and unhappy. Frequent violence in the city had virtually restricted him to the compound after school, where he would hit a ball against the wall for hours. Medical care was uncertain with the best hospital closed, frequent water shortages and electrical blackouts made life unpleasant, and protests by farmers had resulted in food shortages. Alicia had not wanted to leave, but finally she had been swayed by Ben and Salamone's insistence that Addis Ababa at that time was no place for women and children. Yona and I decided to stay.

We took them to the airport during a week when three close friends left as well. Saying good-bye had become a depressingly familiar ritual.

8

SOUNDS OF CHANGE

At the time of my marriage to Jack, I had been excited by the prospect of being able to explore, over time, the Ethiopian musical worlds around me and to gain the intimate knowledge so difficult to achieve during the traditional cycle of a year in the field. But by early 1975 time itself had become an enemy and the revolution directly threatened our future in Ethiopia. A knowledge of Ethiopian languages, history, and culture would be of little use if I could not continue to do research in the country.

While in graduate school, I had heard what I then considered to be apocryphal tales of individuals who had in some way "lost" their fields, prevented by circumstance or proclamation from completing their work or from returning in the future. Now there seemed every possibility that I would join their number. Still, while the general instability in Ethiopia had eliminated the possibility of pursuing rural research, there were opportunities for work in Addis Ababa. When I decided to remain with Jack in Ethiopia after the departure of Alicia and Aviva in early March 1975, I also decided to use whatever time was left to learn as much as I could of the broader spectrum of Ethiopian musical life.

Through the spring and summer of 1974, I had already begun to follow more closely the diverse musical life in Addis Ababa. From the beginning I had been interested in the activities of Orchestra Ethiopia, the ensemble of musicians recruited from all over the country under the emperor's patronage and brought to Addis Ababa to constitute a national folklore ensemble. The group rehearsed in a building at the Haile Selassie I University and performed for both public and private functions in the capital. The orchestra was headed by a young musician trained at a leading music conservatory in the United States and at the Yared School in Addis Ababa, a music school that incorporated studies in Western and Ethiopian music.

Occasionally I attended Orchestra Ethiopia rehearsals, and soon I began to study the *krar*, a six-stringed lyre, with one of the musicians. I ordered my own *krar*, a modern version with a sound box made of a large metal bowl covered on the top with leather, from an instrument maker in the Mercato.

Of particular interest to me at the time were the problems the ensemble encountered in blending solo musicians familiar with many different regional styles into a Western-style orchestra. Most Ethiopian instrumentalists were accustomed to freedom of interpretation. Having to perform as one member of a large group both highlighted regional differences in tuning and style and limited their chances to improvise.

In an effort to solve these problems, which were leading to discordant performances and personal confrontations, the orchestra leaders decided to design a system of musical notation. In this way, they hoped to standardize performance and shape a new, truly national musical idiom. Their new system of musical notation was a remarkable synthesis of symbols derived from Ethiopian church notation and Western musical notation. Numbers were used to indicate the exact pitch that should be played within each of the four standard tuning systems. To guide the musicians in aspects of tempo, rhythm, and interpretation, the leaders drew up a special and rather droll list of pictographs, associating each with a musical activity. A small turtle placed above the notation indicated that the tempo should slow down, while a drawing of a closed door indicated the end of a section of music. A musician was free to ornament only those pitches marked by a small bee hovering above.

By spring 1975, I began to pay attention to other traditions that I had earlier overlooked, taking advantage of every opportunity that arose. It soon became obvious that the course of the revolution could be charted as well in image and sound, and that these symbols were often manipulated to express the significant political issues of the day.

Some of the first changes could be viewed on Ethiopian television, which had formerly carried an eclectic assortment of documentaries, musical entertainment, news, and American reruns. Although its range was limited to the capital and the immediately surrounding areas, during the early months of the revolution the airwaves had been used as a powerful device for reshaping public opinion of Haile Selassie and his regime. In early September 1974, the airing of the graphic British documentary on the 1972 famine set the stage for deposing the emperor.

A new wave of special programs began to dominate revolutionary Ethiopian television, displacing foreign favorites like "Hawaii Five-0," shows that were abruptly abandoned as symbols of capitalist decadence. Performances by urban theatrical and musical ensembles were aired, many dramatizing the successes of the nascent revolution. One early effort featured "Mother Ethiopia," at first shown ill in bed, reduced by feudal graft and malfeasance to a weakened shadow of her former self. A young military officer dressed in a smart khaki uniform enters her room and orders her from her sickbed, accompanied by the chanted invocations of a priest in the background. At the end, Mother Ethiopia miraculously recovers her vitality and joins in the rousing chorus, backed by the singers and instrumentalists of Orchestra Ethiopia.

Song was also a powerful medium for transmitting information about the important policy changes implemented by the PMAC. Governmental authorities first nationalized the private radio station, the missionary-run Radio Voice of the Gospel, which had broadcast religious messages and primarily Western music for many years. It was used by the government, along with the two other state radio stations, as an important vehicle for disseminating revolutionary information. We frequently heard recordings of the song "Ethiopia Tikdem" ("Ethiopia Forward"), the musical embodiment of the central revolutionary motto. The song, a rousing march sung in unison by an enthusiastic chorus of children, set forth goals for the common good.

New radio programs were instituted in important regional languages and well-known musicians of each area were enlisted to sing about revolutionary progress in a traditional musical style. By the end of March 1975, famous *azmari* were singing regularly on the radio in Oromo and other languages about the significance of rural land reforms, accompanying themselves on the *masenqo*.

The radio also provided an intriguing perspective on superpower relations in the ongoing revolutionary process. During early 1975, the most prominent foreign influence was that of the mainland Chinese, who arrived en masse to guide the Ethiopian experience in the footsteps of Mao. Suddenly, Chinese were seen throughout the piazza, crowding hotels, restaurants, and local shops. Ethiopian television ran features about Chinese collective farms, which were held up as models for similar ventures to be introduced shortly in the south. Chinese medical practitioners introduced acupuncture into both urban and rural areas, and radio talk shows carried interviews with villagers who had been treated by these "barefoot doctors."

Testimonials to the benefits of acupuncture were aired in live interview programs, with interviewers randomly asking villagers detailed questions about their treatments. One woman described at length the treatment she had received to alleviate pain in her legs and her problems with walking.

"And how are you doing?" asked the interviewer, in full expectation of a positive response.

"My legs are better now," the woman answered enthusiastically. "But," she continued, oblivious to the thousands who listened, "now I have trouble going to the bathroom!"

Around the same time, the Chinese presence was also reflected in a changing musical repertory. During early 1975, Ethiopian radio began to play recordings of Chinese operas. Ethiopians went about their daily lives with the music of the Red Detachment of Women blaring in the background, the libretti readily available in English translation in local bookshops. But shortly thereafter, the sudden advent of Soviet influence and the arrival of Soviet advisors swept the Chinese away and replaced Chinese opera with stirring recordings by the Red Army Chorus. A competition for a new Ethiopian anthem held in mid-1975 selected as the winner a song resembling an Eastern European folktune, composed by an Ethiopian musician who had received musical training in Bulgaria.

In early February 1975, shortly after the nationalization of the radio station, I received a call from a foreign journalist working at Radio Voice of the Gospel who knew of my interests in Ethiopian music. The future of the station's extensive archives was unclear, he told me. Would I like to select items of particular interest and receive copies of the recordings?

I grabbed a supply of blank tapes and spent the rest of the day at the station looking through the list of holdings. The archives were a treasury of the Ethiopian musical universe. There were recordings of the Imperial Bodyguard Orchestra, organized in the early 1950s by order of Haile Selassie to play Western favorites as well as arrangements of Ethiopian folksongs. The Haile Selassie I Theatre Ensemble, which performed traditional music in an updated style, was also amply represented.

Looking through the files, I was startled to see that there was a single example on tape sung by the *lalibela*, an obscure group of musicians who suffered from leprosy or who were descended from families marked by the stigma of Hansen's disease. The *lalibela* hid their identities, wrapping their white cotton cloaks over their faces. They would arrive around dawn outside the gates of a prosperous compound and begin singing loud verses of praise to the owner. If their song was not quickly rewarded with money or food, they would next sing insults even louder. Although the *lalibela* frequented the urban areas where there were many potential patrons, none had ever come to sing outside our large apartment building in the middle of downtown Addis Ababa.

I asked to hear the *lalibela* example on the spot. The music was indeed as distinctive as their persona: I heard a raucous duet, a woman repeating a wordless refrain while a man improvised the texts of praise. A couple of months later, I was able to meet and interview *lalibela*; I found out that the singers were usually husband and wife, both descended from families stigmatized by leprosy but themselves without infection.

"Look at us, we are clean," said the *lalibela* with whom I spoke. But he made it abundantly clear that the baby his wife held in her arms would maintain their tradition and that he would likely someday appear at dawn with his own wife, his *shamma* wrapped tightly so as to ensure his anonymity, singing the songs of his ancestors. Had the revolution in any way affected their tradition, I asked? "Oh no," the *lalibela* replied. "Business is very good these days."

In my rush to explore all parts of the musical landscape, I began once again to consider studying the music of the Ethiopian church. Although I had earlier attended church services on a number of occasions, I had not systematically pursued research in that area. Since mid-1974, the restrictive curfews had also made it increasingly difficult to attend church rituals. The *Deggwa,* or hymnary, the central musical tradition of the Ethiopian liturgy, generally begins after midnight in the city, giving way in the early morning hours to performance of the Mass. The curfews restricting travel from mid-evening until 6:00 A.M. meant that one had to arrive at the church well before the *Deggwa* began and to remain there the entire night. Spending the night in a church during the best of times was an uncomfortable option for a foreign woman. But given the volatile situation in the city, to do so without any possibility of returning home in the face of an emergency seemed potentially unsafe.

These were not the only considerations. During the early days of the revolution, the church was in a most delicate position, its powerful role throughout Ethiopian history requiring that it be controlled but not completely destroyed. Thus the new members of the PMAC could pledge their loyalty in the name of both "the oppressed masses and the Almighty God," and they could promise to preserve the magnificent architecture, illuminated manuscripts, paintings, and ritual objects of the church. At the same time, their original thirteen-point revolutionary agenda, released in early July 1974, called for "the abolition of certain traditional beliefs and customs which may hamper the unity and progress of Ethiopia." The church, with its centuries of fealty to the Ethiopian emperor, its powerful role in political life, and its clear association with Christian-Amhara hegemony, represented a potential threat to the new regime seeking to dissolve tribal and religious divisions among Ethiopians.

The proclamation nationalizing all rural land in March 1975 destroyed the church's economic base, cutting off the income from its vast lands and eliminating its direct control over the lives of the faithful. This action also accelerated the changes already underway in the lives of the clergy, who were under increasing pressure to use their extensive educational backgrounds and literacy in education, government, and business.

I had made contact with church officials earlier in my stay and had an audience with the Ethiopian patriarch, for which I prepared nervously, reading extensively about church history and liturgy. When I was presented to the patriarch, an impressive man in a long, dark robe, he greeted me warmly and asked where I was from.

"Dallas," I replied, startled by the unexpected personal question.

"I was in Dallas once," he responded enthusiastically, "where I spent an hour when my plane landed." We spent the rest of the interview talking about the Dallas airport, which I suspected throughout had actually been Dulles Airport in Washington, D.C. What, after all, would the Ethiopian patriarch have been doing in Dallas, Texas?

Not long after my interview with the patriarch, new and restrictive guidelines for visiting scholars were introduced, requiring researchers to be accompanied by government-approved "assistants" in their excursions to the field. Permission was rarely given for new ethnographic projects, and work in certain areas was highly suspect. Musical studies did not seem to arouse suspicion, particularly when carried out informally in the capital, but it did not appear to be an appropriate moment to seek formal permission to study Ethiopian Christian music and liturgy.

My new identity as a Shelemay had also subtly altered my relationship to the Ethiopian Christian world. I had earlier introduced myself as an American scholar who was studying *zema*, the name by which the music of both the Ethiopian Christians and Falasha was called. My own background as an American Jew was not generally a subject of interest or discussion. However, I was to learn later that the distinction between being Jewish and being Israeli was confusing to many in the traditional church, in part because the Ethiopian words for Jew and Israelite blurred such religious and national boundaries. With the close relations between Ethiopia and Israel now shattered and the church itself in jeopardy, I and the family were concerned that a Shelemay woman's interest in and attendance at church might in some way arouse comment or even suspicion. So when Father Marqos offered a novel solution to the practical and personal problems inherent in a study of Ethiopian Christian musical tradition, I readily accepted.

In late May 1975, just as the clouds began to thicken over the capital and the big rains were again about to start, Father Marqos brought Marigeta Yohannes to my apartment for tea. Yohannes was an imposing man with a barrel chest, stocky, and well over six feet in height. Dressed in a well-tailored Western sports jacket, tie, and slacks, this master Ethiopian Christian musician embodied aspects of both tradition and modernization in the Ethiopian church.

Trained as a child by his father and grandfather, he progressed in traditional Ethiopian schooling in a local church school near his natal village in the north, learning to read, write, and chant the Praise of Mary. After mastering the reading of the Book of Psalms, he left to study liturgical music and dance at the Bethlehem Monastery, the most famous site for church musical training in the country.

The Bethlehem Monastery, yet another spot reflecting in its name the Ethiopian attachment to the Holy Land, was of great antiquity. Its central importance in the teaching of Ethiopian chant dated from the sixteenth century: it is said to have been the one place where a notated hymnary survived the devastating Muslim invasion that nearly destroyed the empire. The chant tradition was revived at Bethlehem, and beginning in the seventeenth century, its practitioners were patronized by the Ethiopian emperors in their new capital at Gondar. The musicians of Bethlehem came to play an increasingly important role in the perpetuation of the church musical tradition.

The Bethlehem Monastery sits amid the mountains of the northwestern Ethiopian plateau, some forty kilometers south of the small provincial town of Debre Tabor. Below the large, round church where the liturgy is performed, numerous small huts with thatched roofs dot the hillside, providing shelter for students who aspire to learn the chant tradition.

At the height of its influence, the monastery housed as many as two hundred boys, some as young as ten years of age. They studied the *Deggwa* and other service books during the day, beginning to copy out their own manuscripts, based on those of their teachers, on their own parchment. After dusk, they acquired the oral tradition, testing their memory of the melodies at night when none could see the written texts nor follow the guidance of the native system of musical notation. Daily they watched, listened, and eventually participated in performance of the liturgy.

Between classes and services, some of the young musicians-in-training would assist their teachers with chores and household tasks. Wrapped in white cotten shawls, others would walk over the rough trails to nearby markets and villages to beg for food or supplies, which they would bring back to the monastery or, on occasion, resell. To be a musician in Ethiopia, even within the church, inevitably meant being a mendicant, particularly during student days.

Yohannes trained for years at Bethlehem and later became a *marigeta*, a leader of the other *debtera*. But in the mid-1960s, he was called to Addis Ababa to teach at the newly established Theological College, where he began to develop new methods to transmit the traditional church music in an urban academic setting. When we first met during late May 1975, Yohannes was no longer teaching at the college, which had been closed since the early days of the revolution, but he still officiated at his own church in the center of the city.

Over tea, Father Marqos explained to Yohannes that I wished to learn about Ethiopian church music and that I needed a teacher. Marigeta Yohannes agreed to come to my home most afternoons for sessions several hours long, and we set an hourly rate at which I would compensate him for his time. He approved my plans to record all of our sessions, aware that I someday hoped to write about his musical tradition.

We began to work in early June 1975, with Yohannes arriving most days in the mid-afternoon and staying until a little before the dinner hour. We sat in the living room, each in a deep, beige corduroy chair pulled up close to a low, round wooden coffee table on which I had placed a small tape recorder and microphone. Most days we were joined by Tamrat, the student who had earlier helped me to transcribe and translate sections from the Falasha liturgical tapes. Tamrat had returned from Zemetcha and was glad again to have employment, helping to translate and clarify Yohannes's explanations, which were often very technical and well beyond my Amharic competence. Occasionally, the noise of city traffic would intrude, and we would pause while a truck or car passed. Sometimes, the call of the *muezzin* from the adjacent mosque could be heard, establishing an accidental polyphony with Yohannes's chant. After an hour or two, Haddas would bring down a tray of hot tea and homemade cookies, her heavy footsteps on the wooden stairs being the signal to take a break.

I prepared a series of topics and questions for the first sessions with Yohannes, as I always had for field interviews, hoping that his answers would help me understand this mysterious and beautiful tradition. I soon discarded my guidelines, for this master teacher clearly had in mind his own systematic program to lead me through the complicated maze that was Ethiopian chant.

"We will begin," he explained solemnly, "with the regular Sundays, next do the annual holidays, and then cover all other special liturgical occasions. If you like, we can also talk about *qene* (a genre of liturgical poetry) and the *Qeddase* (Mass). But first we will discuss Saint Yared."

Saint Yared, the mythical founder of the Ethiopian chant tradition, is said to have lived during the reign of a sixth-century emperor, Gabra Masqal. According to Ethiopian oral traditions, Yared was the prototypical slow learner and struggled as a student. One day, terribly discouraged, he sat under a tree and watched a caterpillar trying over and over to climb up the trunk, each time losing its grip and tumbling to the ground. But persisting, the caterpillar at last succeeded, and with this model in mind, so did Yared. He became an expert *debtera* and was said to have been visited by the Holy Spirit in the form of a dove, who transmitted to him the entire body of church music. Many Ethiopian paintings show Saint Yared sitting reflectively as a dove brings the sacred chant to his ear from God.

Marigeta Yohannes recounted other stories about Saint Yared, bringing to life images often encountered in Ethiopian paintings and iconography. One such image shows Yared in a white turban and liturgical robe with a border of gold, with his sistrum and prayer staff, performing before Emperor Gabra Masqal. The emperor looks alarmed, for he has just noticed that he has unwittingly stabbed Yared in the foot with his spear. But the musician continues to dance, so transfigured by his music that he does not feel the pain. Legend has it that the emperor, moved by this experience, told Yared that he would grant him anything he desired. To the emperor's great surprise, the musician asked only to be allowed to leave the court and live in isolation.

There are other traditions about Saint Yared that Yohannes did not recount that were told to me by the Beta Israel. One knowledgeable Falasha elder insisted that Yared's mother was a member of the Falasha community. Others transmitted the tradition that Yared came from the high Semien Mountains, where many Falasha once lived. One tale even suggests that an icy place where Yared used to pray became a place of pilgrimage for members of the Beta Israel community. Yet despite their familiarity with Saint Yared, the Falasha did not credit him with composing their liturgical music.

It was only the Bethlehem Monastery that claimed to perpetuate the style of Saint Yared himself. As one of the expert Bethlehem musicians sustaining this heritage, Yohannes sang in a strong, resonant voice of great range and expressiveness. Over the months he performed hundreds of chants, explaining their musical settings and place in the liturgical cycle. By October, we had recorded the most important musical portions for the liturgical year, devoting many hours as well to discussion of the lives and careers of Yared's heirs.

We never discussed one provocative aspect of many *debtera'* lives—their frequent involvement in traditional medicine and magical practice. Marigeta Yohannes never volunteered information and, knowing the subject to be sensitive, I never asked directly. It was widely acknowledged that during their years of training many *debtera* learned to make amulets, long thin strips of parchment filled with invocations and prayers written in ink. Many are decorated with small geometrical drawings and rough pictures of Ethiopian saints thought to have the capacity to ward off the evil eye and other spirits that cause illness and misfortune. Any interested young *debtera* can learn a few standard texts of this type, which they can recopy and sell for income. But over time, some *debtera* would concentrate on these magical activities, expanding their output from making copies to producing original, sometimes ornate, amulets to cure certain illnesses or to exorcise particular spirits. Some amulets would be decorated with the image of Saint Michael holding his sword, perhaps surrounded by a border of small, black eyes to ward off the evil eye.

As his liturgical training increases, a musician may become further expert at oral therapies, which require him to invoke and "pull" the spirits sickening a patient and then to offer a cure through recitation of prayers and herbal remedies. Here, sanctioned liturgical performance becomes magic, the unauthorized use of sacred Ethiopian Christian texts to exorcise spirits of various origins.

Over the months, our work became the anchor that held me steady amid the chaos that was engulfing both my personal and professional worlds. Marigeta Yohannes, too, I believe, welcomed our daily sessions for more than the monetary payment he received. He was under enormous stress as a clergyman and as a human being, pressures that would immediately surface whenever we turned off the tape recorder and just talked over tea. No doubt, too, he valued the opportunity to share his extraordinary knowledge of a tradition increasingly devalued within his own society.

The many hours spent with Marigeta Yohannes filled my days and soothed my agitation. I was once again in close contact with an Ethiopian musician who became both a teacher and a friend. But reaching out to Marigeta Yohannes had a further impact I could not have anticipated at the time—it forever altered my perspective on the Beta Israel.

9

UNEXPECTED FINDINGS

After completing my work with Marigeta Yohannes in fall 1975, I returned to my neglected doctoral dissertation. The revolution had led me away from my focus on Falasha liturgical music into a rich array of different materials. For most of 1975, I had escaped the mounting pressures around me by carrying out new research. This activity enabled me to reach out and remain in touch, however tentatively, with the broader Ethiopian world around me. The demands of the research process also provided a welcome release from the all-consuming political tension in Ethiopia, while not requiring the same intense level of concentration that would be necessary to prod my dissertation along. During 1975 I gathered data almost on automatic pilot, stimulated by the challenge of the new and relieved of the pressure to move constantly deeper into questions of interpretation.

My research on the Ethiopian Christian tradition left me newly aware of the broad similarities between it and the Falasha tradition in language, music, and aesthetics. Both liturgies had prayer texts in the Ge'ez language, used similar melodies repeated for many verses, and utilized a drum and another percussion instrument to provide regular rhythmic accompaniment. But the crisis that had led me to seek new fields of inquiry also left me unable to explore these new insights or to relate them to what I had done before. The revolution, while inadvertently moving me in new directions, had so upset my equilibrium that some time had to pass before I could realize what I had in hand.

Using the musical and textual transcriptions I had completed in 1974, I finished a doctoral thesis in the United States in 1977. Still I was left with a sense that my work on the Beta Israel was unfinished, that I had not delved deeply enough into the extraordinary materials I had gathered. Only in the spring of 1978 did a new picture emerge, with sudden and overwhelming clarity.

In the months after receiving my Ph.D., I completed additional musical and textual transcriptions from the entire liturgical cycle, which, along with those done for the dissertation, provided an overview of these seemingly impenetrable rituals. Next I compared the long hours of ritual recorded in the Falasha prayerhouse with the individual prayers sung and discussed by priests during interviews. In this manner, I slowly identified some twenty-seven prayers that together provided the framework for the Falasha liturgy. Many were common to all rituals, providing a fixed structure within which other special prayers for a given holiday could be interpolated. All of the holiday morning services began with the same prayer, its words changing slightly to reflect the day at hand. This and other prayers became familiar guideposts in the lengthy rituals—for example, a rousing rendition of All the Angels Cried Out, a morning prayer that recounted the manner in which angels in the "seventh heaven" praised God. Likewise, most evening services began with Blessed Be the Lord, a prayer praising the Lord God of Israel, in the name of all the biblical fathers.

On the Sabbath and *Seged* there were long renditions of a prayer that began "Come, let us worship," calling the faithful to bow and praise God. In sum, the more than fifty hours of annual holiday, Sabbath, daily, and other rituals I had recorded among the Falasha in 1973 were remarkably consistent in their content and order. The Beta Israel liturgy had unity and coherence, each ritual linked to the others through shared text and music.

Where had this extraordinary liturgical tradition come from? Though I felt that I had finally succeeded in assembling the pieces of a giant jigsaw puzzle, and though I watched the many pieces combine to form a coherent image, the image did not match the picture on the puzzle's box. That picture was of a Jewish religious and liturgical tradition preserved for millennia, assumed to have been introduced to Ethiopia before Christianity's fourth-century adoption by the court. The Beta Israel were thought to have sustained this religious practice in the ensuing centuries, untouched by the outside world, as the residue of an otherwise lost Jewish past.

I did not at first explicitly question, on a theoretical basis, this unlikely vision of an isolated and static religious tradition. But I could see that the Falasha rituals with which I was working had little resemblance to normative Jewish liturgy, even to a tradition that might have been formed long before the modern era. There was no regular, weekly reading of a portion of the Five Books of Moses in the Falasha liturgy, an important part of universal Jewish practice from earliest dates. I could find only the most fragmentary similarities to the major Jewish prayers. For instance, one Falasha prayer resembles the Jewish *Kedushah,* the Thrice Holy, while a line from another parallels a section of the Jewish *Kaddish,* the Sanctification. Both of these Falasha texts, which at first glance appear to derive from Jewish models, are also found in the modern Ethiopian Christian liturgy in a form that more closely resembles the Beta Israel prayers than those in Jewish practice.

The central creedal statement of Jewish tradition, the *Shema,* is missing altogether from Falasha worship except for one brief reference in the Sabbath liturgy, embedded within a prayer of praise. One verse of this Sabbath prayer proclaims: "Hear, Israel, the commandments of God; Adonay is one, his name is his alone." Like so much of the rest of Falasha tradition, this prayer points at once in two directions. While its wording deviates from that of the Hebrew creed derived from Deuteronomy 6:4–5, it certainly contains an unequivocal acknowledgment of belief in one God as well as a nod to Jewish custom. But this same Beta Israel prayer also contains a verse from Psalm 145 that is used at a critical point in the Ethiopian Christian Mass, where it is sung four times after Communion: "My mouth shall speak the praise of Adonay. Let all flesh bless his holy name." And, what is equally striking, this Beta Israel Sabbath prayer is sung to a melody widely used in Ethiopian Christian rituals.

In short, virtually every parallel to Jewish tradition that I was able to find in the Beta Israel liturgy is also present in the prayers of the Ethiopian Orthodox church. In contrast, the major elements of Jewish liturgy known to have been part of universal Jewish practice for nearly two millennia are simply not present in Beta Israel prayer.

My experience with Ethiopian Christian liturgy also led me into a new world of scholarship about Christian liturgy and chant. I had earlier studied only Jewish practice and liturgy, the seemingly obvious path for one interested in studying the Beta Israel. But my new awareness of Ethiopian Christian practice suggested that the Falasha liturgy contains a number of prayers and forms found only in Christian tradition. In virtually every Beta Israel ritual, the priests perform the Canticle of the Three Youths in the Fire, an apocryphal text drawn from the Book of Daniel. This prayer, of great importance in Ethiopian Christian tradition as well as in Christian worship universally, was never accepted into Jewish canon or ritual. I found other prayers of Ethiopian Christian origin in all Beta Israel rituals, as well as quotations and paraphrases from the New Testament.

I was left with questions that I could not answer. How did the Falasha come to transmit this distinctive liturgy, so strong in Jewish sentiment yet lacking the most important Jewish liturgical elements? Likewise, why did this liturgy share so much in both form and content with the Ethiopian Christian liturgy while at the same time omit the important creedal sections of Christian ritual?

The answers were actually quite simple and were provided by the Beta Israel themselves. Scholars before me had been so busy weaving their own theories based on assumptions about the way things must have been that they had not looked closely enough at the evidence before them. I had nearly made the same mistake and had, in addition, neglected to listen from the outset to what the Beta Israel had to say about their own past. I think now that there must have been several reasons for my tunnel vision—my inexperience, the distractions of the revolution, the amount of time required to gain control over the materials I had collected. But fortunately, the new data I gathered in Falasha villages came to serve as a corrective to the assumptions I had tacitly held. Perhaps equally important, I had been trained in a discipline that tends to value the testimony of the people who transmit a cultural tradition. In contrast, the scholarly explanations long accepted as fact not only did not provide answers to these questions, they had led to a dead end. This was the position in which I found myself by the end of 1975, although it took me several years more to move beyond a vague discomfort concerning the lack of fit between what I "knew" and what I saw in the data before me.

One night in March 1978, as I was preparing a paper for a major Ethiopian studies conference, I arrived at an impasse. When one reaches a dead end in scholarship, the way out is often found by returning to the primary information itself, searching for clues somehow missed or overlooked. I had not gone over my field materials since I had completed my dissertation the previous August and moved to New York to begin my teaching career. I decided that I should now take a close look at the transcripts I had earlier made of all my interviews with the Beta Israel priests.

One particular interview had long puzzled me, and I lingered for some time over it, listening to the tape recording and rereading the transcript. Alaqa Gete, the former head priest of the Ambober area, had talked to me at length about the monks who had once headed the Falasha clergy. The monks had largely died out by the 1970s, their formerly powerful role in Falasha religion weakened and ultimately destroyed primarily by the growing identification of their community with the Jewish world abroad. But like almost all the other priests I met, Alaqa Gete had studied with the monks as a child. From them he had acquired the knowledge of the Ge'ez language that had gained him the respect of his fellow priests throughout his life.

Alaqa Gete remembered that the monks had once prayed seven times a day—twice during the night, at sunrise, three times during the day, and at sunset. These prayer services were the "hours" of the monastic office, also referred to as "the keeping of the time." Alaqa Gete could still recall the beginnings of each of the hours, and he sang them for me. Though I was fascinated that he remembered portions of the monastic office, I was not greatly surprised to learn that the Beta Israel monks, like their cohorts in Ethiopian Christian practice, had prayed seven times a day. After all, the Beta Israel credited a fifteenth-century Ethiopian Christian monk, Abba Sabra, with bringing monasticism to their community. Abba Sabra was also said to have introduced many other aspects of their religious practice, ranging from the annual calendar to the laws of isolation. But, like everyone before me, I had long ago filed away Alaqa Gete's discussion of monasticism as well as the monastic prayers he performed, and I continued to view Falasha monasticism as a relatively late (fifteenth-century) Christian influence on the preexisting Jewish fabric of Beta Israel religious life.

Now I returned to the words of Alaqa Gete and his memories of Falasha monks with a new perspective—I had become quite familiar with the prayers that provided the substance of most Beta Israel prayerhouse rituals. One Beta Israel priest, surprised at my knowledge of a liturgy known only to the increasingly aged clergy, remarked that in twenty-five years only I would remember the Beta Israel prayers. Although others had translated Falasha prayers from manuscripts, I was the first to have studied the complete liturgy, along with its musical content, as performed orally in the prayerhouse.

As I read over the transcripts of Alaqa Gete's interviews, and listened to my recordings of his renditions of the prayers that began each of the seven monastic prayer services, I drew in my breath sharply. I realized that *I knew these prayers already*—they were the major prayers of the liturgy with which I had been working for years. With increasing excitement, I realized that the first prayer of the monastic office, performed at sunset, was Blessed Be the Lord, the prayer that begins the evening prayerhouse rituals. Slowly, I reviewed Alaqa Gete's list of monastic prayers, realizing that almost every prayer he sang was still performed in the modern prayerhouse liturgy at the same point at which it had occurred in monastic practice. The evidence before me was quite unequivocal: the office was not a separate order of service that had died with the Falasha monks; rather, it was the core of the modern Falasha liturgy.

The implications of this finding stunned me. Because of the many Jewish aspects of Falasha religion—most notably the observance of a Saturday Sabbath, other corollaries to several major Jewish holidays, the strongly expressed monotheism—most earlier scholars had assumed that the entire Falasha religious tradition and liturgy had been obtained directly from an external Jewish source and somehow preserved by the Beta Israel for two thousand years. But if that were the case, then the Beta Israel prayerhouse liturgy would necessarily be of Jewish origin, with Jewish liturgical content, separate and distinct from the monastic office brought by the Christian monks, who joined the community over one thousand years later. At the very least, one would expect to find major hallmarks of Jewish liturgy, even if overlaid with monastic influence. Yet what I had before me was a single liturgical tradition, the one credited by the Beta Israel themselves to the influence of Ethiopian Christian monks of the late Middle Ages. There was no old Jewish liturgy, only an Ethiopian liturgical tradition sharing the language, liturgical texts and orders, and even the music of the Ethiopian church.

Once I grasped the evidence from within the Falasha tradition itself, I was able to begin to explore its broader implications. The pervasive impact of Jewish and biblical custom on many aspects of general Ethiopian Christian culture had already been documented in great detail by others, most notably by Edward Ullendorff in *Ethiopia and the Bible* (1968). Ethiopian Christians, too, had observed a Saturday Sabbath throughout much of their history, had maintained a prohibition against eating pork, and had practiced the rite of circumcision. Lacking any firm evidence for the source of these Jewish influences on Ethiopian Christianity, some scholars speculated that Jews from southern Arabia might have brought them to Ethiopia. Since there was little likelihood that Judaism could have either so heavily influenced Ethiopian Christianity or become so widely dispersed in Ethiopia after Christianity became the official state religion in the fourth century, most had also concluded that such a pervasive Jewish influence could only have occurred at an earlier date. Yet whatever the source of the presumed early Jewish impact on Ethiopia, it had cut a wide swath through a range of Ethiopian religious traditions, leaving an indelible mark on Ethiopian Christianity. The Falasha could therefore not be approached as an isolated Jewish tradition within a Christian empire. Furthermore, extensive work by literary scholars had already concluded that the Beta Israel had received their written literature, including the *Orit*, from Ethiopian Christian sources, most of it as late as the fourteenth and fifteenth centuries. I now was confronted with similar questions about the liturgy and its musical setting.

I began to reread discussions of Ethiopian history and to seek new sources that might provide an explanation for the liturgical materials I had uncovered. Ethiopian emperors from the fourteenth century onward had left historical chronicles, making it possible to reconstruct events during their often turbulent reigns. The Ethiopian church, too, with its strong literary tradition, had supported scribes who recorded tales of an expanding empire where church and state had been inexorably linked for centuries. Both old and newly discovered sources for medieval Ethiopian history, many available in translation, were by the early 1970s being productively mined by Ethiopian historians and linguists who sorted through and expertly interpreted the course of events.

It was in the new studies of Ethiopian history and literature that I found the final key to understanding how the Beta Israel might have come to perpetuate a Judaic tradition that apparently was brought to them by Ethiopian Christian monks. This seeming paradox was actually quite consistent with the religious history of the country. The Ethiopian church had been torn by conflict throughout its documented history, with supporters of its long-standing Judaized tradition under continual pressure from their Alexandrian patriarchs to normalize their tradition with other Eastern Orthodox churches. A period of particularly grave internal conflict took place in the fourteenth and fifteenth centuries, when several Ethiopian monastic groups actually refused to take vows and left the church rather then give up their observance of the Saturday Sabbath and other biblical traditions. These monks dispersed throughout northern Ethiopia. There they founded new monasteries and converted many people not yet under the influence of Ethiopian Christianity. There are many references to these renegade monks in the Ethiopian historical sources of the period. They were often termed *ayhud,* which literally means Jew, an epithet that in medieval Ethiopia referred to heretics or rebels in conflict with the church. These conflicts came to a climax during the reign of Emperor Zar'a Ya'qob, who ruled between 1434 and 1468. At that time, several groups of heretic monks returned at last to the church and observance of both the Saturday and Sunday Sabbaths was sanctioned.

It was plausible, therefore, that the Beta Israel had received not only their prayers but also their biblical and Jewish religious traditions from Ethiopian Christian monks. The most powerful argument for this interpretation was provided by the Beta Israel themselves: they dated the life of the influential Ethiopian Christian monk Abba Sabra to the period of Emperor Zar'a Ya'qob, the emperor whose reign marked the most serious religious controversies. Some Beta Israel oral traditions even mention that Abba Sabra's disciple Sagga Amlak, said to be the son of the emperor, fled the Ethiopian court and joined the Falasha. Perhaps not coincidentally, the name of Emperor Zar'a Ya'qob is found in Falasha prayers recorded in surviving Falasha manuscripts.

Thus several strands of evidence—the music and texts of the Beta Israel liturgy, the oral traditions of the Beta Israel about the history of their religion and prayers, and information from Ethiopian historical sources—together provide a new picture of Falasha religious history. An Ethiopian people, probably of indigenous Agau stock, came into contact with fringe Ethiopian monastic groups in the late Middle Ages and adopted the eclectic Judaic religious tradition that the monks brought with them. These people became part of a larger group of rebels and heretics, many of whom were called *ayhud* by the court and the church. Many of these rebels were later reabsorbed into the church, but some evidently remained separate, including those who became the community called the Beta Israel. Eventually, they gained considerable military strength in the northwest mountains of the highland plateau. Only in the sixteenth century do we find the first historical references to a people called Falasha in the Ethiopian royal chronicles, suggesting that only then were they emerging as a distinctive group. Alongside them today still live other tribes with similar histories, such as the Qemant, who maintain their own distinctive mixture of Agau, Judaic, and Christian traditions.

What was the religion of the Beta Israel like before the arrival of Judaized Ethiopian monks? We may never be able to answer that question with any degree of certainty. Like so many of the groups influenced by the powerful monastic movements of the Ethiopian church, it seems likely that the Falasha originally had their own Agau religion. The modern Beta Israel still transmit Agau language texts within their Ge'ez prayers, some containing the name of the Agau Sky God. But it is also possible that the Beta Israel had had contact with Ethiopian monasticism before the time of Abba Sabra, or perhaps with other earlier Judaic elements in Ethiopia. Such contacts might have laid a foundation for their acceptance of monasticism and the religious reforms of Abba Sabra.

While the source of the early Jewish influence on Ethiopian Christianity remains an enigma, I now had compelling evidence dating the Beta Israel liturgical tradition to the fifteenth century, over a millennium after the entry of Christianity into Ethiopia. Whatever the early Jewish influence on Ethiopia, there was scant evidence that the surviving Beta Israel liturgy directly reflected its form or content.

Very few experiences match the joy of solving an intractable intellectual problem. For an ethnomusicologist who seeks to explore music in its cultural context, to be able to cast new light on history at large is a surprising and gratifying development. But along with my excitement at the strength of this new historical theory came a new set of problems: I had arrived at conclusions that few outside the scholarly world wished to hear. Although my work was greeted enthusiastically by many in Ethiopian studies and musical scholarship, the activists who had worked for years to ensure recognition of the Beta Israel as Jews and to aid their eventual immigration to Israel did not welcome my findings. After years of trying to avoid entering the often acrimonious political and religious debates about Falasha religious identity, I was thrust into the center of the controversy with dramatic new evidence.

When Joseph Halévy first visited Falasha villages in the mid-1860s, the people he encountered did not consider themselves to be Jews—they told Halévy that they were the Beta Israel, the House of Israel. Shocked to hear that others elsewhere shared their traditions, they were even more overwhelmed when Halévy himself claimed to be a Falasha. The subsequent century of increasingly close contact greatly altered the Beta Israel's self-perception. By the time I arrived in Ethiopia, most of the Falasha community identified with Jews of the outside world who for decades had been increasingly active on their behalf. Following the lead of American organizations who championed their cause, by the mid-1970s they had begun to call themselves Ethiopian Jews, discarding their traditional tribal names, Beta Israel and Falasha, as embarrassing reminders of their past. From the beginning I sympathized with the predicament of the modern Beta Israel, caught between both worlds and forced to make a choice.

In 1973, the chief Sephardic rabbi of Israel recognized the Falasha as Jews, declaring them descendants of the Tribe of Dan. His ruling provided the legal basis for the Falasha to be eligible to move to Israel under the Law of Return. Almost immediately, Western supporters mobilized and began an active campaign to help the Beta Israel emigrate. But just as the official barriers to Ethiopian Jewish immigration were falling, Ethiopia broke its long-standing and close relations with Israel during the autumn of 1973, in the aftermath of the Yom Kippur War. Although the emperor had earlier dismissed foreign requests for free Falasha emigration, stating that the Falasha were an old and important part of Ethiopian society, the break in relations introduced a new, seemingly insurmountable barrier.

During 1974, efforts intensified to make possible Falasha emigration. As the Ethiopian revolution began and possibilities of negotiation on the subject became even more problematic, Jewish organizations began to help individuals and small groups of Ethiopian Jews to leave the country. Some American activists traveled to Ethiopia, posing as tourists while actually working to facilitate Falasha emigration. On a number of occasions they crossed the bounds of legality and risked direct confrontation with the Ethiopian authorities. I was concerned about their personal welfare as well as the legal and political implications of their activities for the Beta Israel. One particularly reckless visitor cut a wide swath through government circles, paid off a number of well-placed officials, and somehow managed to leave the country safely, several Falasha children in tow. The ends justify the means, I was told by more than one visitor, as we talked over coffee or dinner at my Addis Ababa home.

I liked many of these people personally and came to understand better their almost fanatical commitment to the Beta Israel. Several alluded to guilt over the inability of the American Jewish community to save European Jewry during the Holocaust. The Falasha cause, they felt, was a rare opportunity to in some way compensate for that earlier tragedy, a chance to rescue Jewish lives in jeopardy. Others had been activists in the American civil rights movement. Disillusioned by black radicalism in the 1960s, they had come to view the Ethiopian Jews as a cause that demonstrated their commitment to racial equality.

Many of these individuals were curious about my research and excited to learn more about the mysterious Beta Israel religious tradition. They wanted details about Falasha religious practice and liturgy. Did the Beta Israel read the Torah? What elements of ancient Jewish liturgy did they sustain in their prayerhouse? What musical connections did I find to the traditions of other Jews? Although I had not yet arrived at the dramatic conclusions that were to surface in 1978, I was already aware of the strong ties that linked Beta Israel customs to those of other Ethiopians, a perspective that many of these visitors greeted with consternation or outright disdain. I was frequently admonished for "not giving more attention to what is Jewish in Falasha tradition." I was already uncomfortably close to challenging the deeply held belief that an unchanging, universal Jewish tradition had been sustained by the Beta Israel.

I was also aware that many in the Beta Israel community were now committed to leaving Ethiopia. When I visited Gondar area villages in 1973, well before the instability of the revolution and subsequent drought and famine, I found many Beta Israel already talking of moving to Israel. One Ambober family had left some months before my arrival and others had children living in Israel. Ambober teachers who had studied in Israel talked frequently about life there, a connection reinforced by the occasional arrival of Jewish visitors from abroad. I was sometimes asked to help villagers get money or obtain the necessary papers for the trip, actions well beyond the influence and resources of a graduate student. Whatever the realities of their history, it seemed clear that the future of this community would be in Israel.

Thus when I finally arrived, in 1978, at an understanding of the monastic component in Falasha tradition, I knew that my findings posed an ethical dilemma. How could I advance conclusions that, however well supported, might cause distress or even be used against the very people who had trusted me with their traditions? Colleagues with whom I discussed the matter were equally stumped at how to handle the situation. I tried to discuss my findings with members of the Beta Israel community with whom I was still able to communicate, in the hope that their response might provide a solution. In 1979, Yosef Berhanu, the longtime liaison between the Beta Israel community and the outside Jewish world, came to New York on a tour to raise money for resettlement of the Ethiopian Jews in Israel. We had an emotional reunion in my New York apartment.

During that evening, I told Ato Yosef about my recent work, explaining that I had become very interested in the influence of

Abba Sabra and the monks upon the Falasha religious tradition. With great enthusiasm, he discussed the impact of monks who were still active in the villages in which he had grown up, early in the century.

"Ato Yosef," I asked at one point, "you credit so many innovations to the monks. I wonder if you have ever considered the possibility that the Falasha prayers surviving today might also have been brought by Abba Sabra and his followers?"

"Oh, no," he answered sharply. "The monks came to us and we converted them."

In 1980, I spent six weeks in Israel working with two Beta Israel priests whom I had earlier interviewed in both Ethiopia and Israel. I inquired at length about Abba Sabra and was greeted with a number of traditional stories about his impact on the Beta Israel community and their religious practice. Both men confirmed that the monks had performed an office seven times a day and each sang the same monastic prayers I had earlier gathered in Ethiopia from Alaqa Gete. As children, both had studied with the monks in their natal villages, and they remembered them with great affection. "The monks in the old days, they taught us everything," one priest recalled. "Only recently they finished because no one wants to be one anymore." And what had Beta Israel religion been like before Abba Sabra came to them? "Before him, all was unclear," the priest responded. Once again, however, the discussion hit the brick wall of their belief that the Falasha had converted Abba Sabra: "Abba Sabra came to the Falashas to convert them to Christianity—he had been the father confessor and teacher of Sagga Amlak, the son of Zar'a Ya'qob. When he arrived to the Falashas, he was converted by them."

Previous scholars who were familiar with Beta Israel oral traditions about the advent of monasticism in their community had accepted this tradition at face value—it was consistent with their assumption that Christian monks had entered into a preexisting Jewish milieu. Yet historical evidence newly available by the late 1970s indicated that the monks who had come to the Beta Israel in the late Middle Ages were intensely devoted to their own traditions, so much so that they had left the church rather than modify their own Judaized beliefs and customs. That they would then arrive at another community and adopt a new religious system simply does not correspond to what is now known of their activities, nor does it explain the survival of so many monastic traditions among the Beta Israel. But I could not bring myself to argue further these points with my research associates and friends. In the end, I presented their views alongside my own interpretations.

Only after some months of soul-searching was I able to decide on a course of action. Though I concluded that I could not conceal what I had discovered because of the current political climate, I did have a responsibility to protect the community with which I had worked. I decided to publish my findings only in scholarly circles and to avoid unnecessary publicity that might inadvertently arouse controversy and damage the Beta Israel. I also stated clearly in all my publications that the data I had uncovered, and my resulting interpretations, should relate only to the past, not to contemporary politics.

This strategy was largely successful. I was able to explore the implications of my findings within a receptive scholarly context while contributing guardedly to an occasional public discussion or benefit on behalf of the Beta Israel. But as the situation in Ethiopia deteriorated with the onset of drought and famine in the mid-1980s, and as efforts to speed the emigration of the Ethiopian Jews therefore accelerated, my involvement with organizations supporting Beta Israel immigration to Israel became increasingly problematic. I was disturbed at the level of hyperbole in their literature, which I knew from reliable sources still in Ethiopia distorted the actual situation. At the same time, a number of individuals working on behalf of the Ethiopian Jews had access to my scholarly work and exerted pressure on me to either withhold the information or modify my conclusions.

By 1986, the tension that had increasingly permeated my personal relationships with the leaders of one activist organization became public when I was invited to guest curate an exhibition on the Ethiopian Jews at the Jewish Museum in New York City. Although we mounted what was generally a well-received exhibition, several individuals protested the representation of the Beta Israel as part of Ethiopian culture, laying the blame at my feet. They demanded that my recently published book, copies of which were on sale in the museum gift shop along with other available writings about the Beta Israel, be removed from the shelves. At an educational event sponsored in conjunction with the exhibition, a small group staged a confrontation, publicly criticizing my findings. I was shocked by this and by the manner in which the critique was orchestrated for political purposes. Additionally, the public nature of this confrontation reinforced my sense that I could no longer remain silent while my work and reputation were attacked by individuals whose cause, despite my ambivalence, I had sought to protect.

Then, too, the Beta Israel community had for some time been firmly established in Israel. Efforts were continuing, through official channels, to facilitate the emigration of those Ethiopian Jews still in Ethiopia who wished to leave. The stabilization of the situation of Ethiopian Jews in Israel had already reduced the possibility that my findings could in any way jeopardize their future. I decided to continue work on this book, setting forth the details of my conclusions, the resulting controversy, and my own changing response to the situation over time.

Although I remain deeply supportive of the future of Ethiopian Jews in Israel, I suspect I will always be troubled by the manner in which Westerners so arrogantly sought—and largely succeeded—to transform these people into mirror images of themselves. The political debate of the late twentieth century over the religious status of the Beta Israel was probably unavoidable, given the long-standing cultural interference by outsiders. A positive result is that the Ethiopian Jews have realized many of their dreams. But in turn, they have become ashamed of their past.

Members of the Beta Israel community have not responded in any formal way to my research, preoccupied with the real-life problems of resettlement, certainly hindered by differences in language and literacy from entering the debate. In 1988, I visited two of the surviving Beta Israel priests in Israel and gave them copies of *Music, Ritual, and Falasha History*. We looked through the book together, and I explained how I had transcribed the music and texts of their prayers. I read each man his own biography, included in an appendix, and I told them that I had written quite a lot about Abba Sabra and the impact of the monks on the Beta Israel community. Both men were delighted to receive the book, although they were unable to read it themselves. Perhaps someday their children or grandchildren will survey all that has been written about their past with a fresh perspective, and will provide a response of their own.

10

A SONG OF LONGING

As the situation in Ethiopia deteriorated during late 1974 and into the early months of 1975, everyone struggled to find means for coping with the increasing tension. Most who could, left, deciding to pick up the pieces of their lives elsewhere; they abandoned businesses, homes, even families. Those who by law or circumstance could not leave turned to friends and drink to defuse the unrelenting tension.

My dreams, ever more frequent, were usually terrifying nightmares. I was unable to concentrate enough to read much, except for one slim paperback out of the hundreds of volumes in our house, a journalistic chronicle of airplane disasters. I found a certain type of morbid comfort in reading about these sudden, violent tragedies, and for several months Jack and I compulsively passed that single book back and forth.

Increasingly isolated and upset, I felt trapped in a crisis about which I could do nothing, my commitment to Jack and Ethiopia pitted against a growing desire for the normalcy that I knew existed just beyond our reach. Our activities had become very constrained, each new event or proclamation further reducing where we could go and even what we could say. My plunge into new research in defiance of the situation had provided some relief, but I needed to reach out, to get some perspective on my place in the world.

One afternoon in early January 1975, I invited several friends over to discuss issues that touched the lives of expatriate women abroad. I suppose my feminism had consciously bloomed one day around my sixteenth birthday, when I told my mother I did not want to become a housewife. Ours was a happy home in Texas, with the traditional roles of my parents underpinning a strong and resilient family relationship. I was the eldest child, one of two girls, and had always had the feeling that my internal compass was set on a course that would incorporate a career.

By the time I came to ethnomusicology and Ethiopia some years later, my development as a woman and an independent professional had not yet caused internal conflicts. Many tried to discourage me from my Ethiopian journey, arguing that a woman would not be able to undertake the projects I had planned. That I had proven them wrong was a great satisfaction. But when I was married in the field, and congratulated by some for "the great prize I had caught on my African safari," I realized that many people thought that I had made a traditional choice.

In part because of this, I had tried to partition my experience, separating that of the scholar from that of the wife, that of the researcher from that of the woman. Then the revolution began and swept away all such distinctions, everyone and everything caught up in its power. I had tried to approach my Ethiopian experience as a series of roles that I had either chosen or been required to play. But I was to discover that, in the end, there was only a frightened American woman behind all the masks, fearful of losing the person and place she loved. The marriage that had at first seemed to compromise my independence and my relationship to Ethiopia now had to be acknowledged as an integral part of my Ethiopian experience. Not only was it inseparable from my perception of the world around me, but it had slowly become a backdrop that provided depth and color. It was by turning to a group of women that I was able to acknowledge this complete if painful whole.

Each of the women I invited to my home on that January day had come to Ethiopia for a different reason, and each had found herself struggling. Susan James, half of the American diplomatic couple whose hospitality had warmed my first weeks in Ethiopia, had left behind her own nascent career in social work for the itinerant life of a foreign service wife and mother. She was just beginning to realize the implications of her choice. Jean Richardson was an ebullient, outspoken Californian, in Ethiopia to do research on public health, whose marriage to an American academic was falling apart under the strains of third-world living. Ann Dorson had come to Ethiopia with the Peace Corps and remained in the capital afterward, in love with a young Ethiopian businessman, undecided whether to stay or leave. Julie Saunders was a tall, angular woman in middle age who had accompanied her husband to a U.N. post in Addis Ababa, abandoning an active life as a museum curator for the challenge of Africa. All of us were linked by time, place, and nationality. We were further joined by the knowledge that the paths we had taken had of necessity excluded other possibilities.

Some weeks we read and discussed feminist literature, at other times we discussed marriage and cross-cultural life-styles, each woman selecting a topic for meetings to be held at her own home. We spoke often of the dilemma of the modern Ethiopian woman, whose very exposure to the education and careers that we valued so highly inevitably excluded her from anything approaching a normal life within her own culture.

For four months we met regularly, extending to each other warmth and honesty, trying to reconcile the tensions inherent in each of our lives. Then Susan's husband was abruptly transferred to his next post and Jean returned to California. Ann, terrified of the violence, went home for a visit to the American South. There, I later learned, she discovered religion. She never returned to Ethiopia or to her lover, writing only that she had asked for and received forgiveness for living in sin in Ethiopia. Only Julie remained, an enigma, occupied with her needlework and crafts, less in Africa than in a world of her own.

When the last pediatrician left the capital in May, my sister-in-law Yona decided that she, too, must depart, afraid for the health of her young daughter. We spent several hectic days preparing for her departure to Israel, searching the increasingly bare shops for a few last gifts, putting the house in order for her husband, Moshe, who would be left behind. Everywhere we went everyone seemed on edge, hysteria lurking just below the surface. One afternoon, as I sat waiting for Yona to complete some last-minute alterations with the one skilled dressmaker left in the capital, I heard voices raised in anger. Suddenly, Yona ran through the doorway, across the veranda where I was sitting, and down the walk to the car. Behind her came slow, fat Eva, waving her sewing shears above her head. I ran to separate the pair, who were threatening to come to blows, one screaming in Hebrew, the other in Armenian. We drove off, with Eva still shouting after us and brandishing her scissors, the altercation evidently provoked by Yona's complaint that a seam was not straight. We drove back toward Benin Sefer, shaken by the silly spat, quietly looking around at the soldiers with automatic weapons on many corners. We stopped at a traffic light midway up the hill and Yona turned to me. "If you think things are difficult now," she said, "just wait. This is only the beginning."

In late July 1975, all land and buildings in urban centers throughout the country were nationalized. Owners of both individual and multiunit buildings were required to register their properties, and all rental income reverted to the government. Owners were allowed to retain the single-family dwelling in which they lived or their own apartment in the building they had previously owned. The Shelemay buildings were now the property of the government, though we each retained the title to our individual flats.

In the wake of the nationalization of urban property, the power of the police force was curtailed and local militias were set up in various districts of the capital. Called *kebele*, these militias were in charge of law and order and enforcing the curfew, which still changed frequently. To be accepted in a *kebele*, a person had to prove that he had never owned land, had limited education, and had earned no more than fifty Ethiopian dollars a month, thus ensuring that no one who had ever held even a modest position of responsibility could play any role.

Armed and empowered to shoot or detain anyone whom they considered to be a counterrevolutionary, as well as to arbitrate or judge disputes, the *kebele* introduced a terrifying new variable into urban life. Frequent gun battles broke out between the militias and their perceived opponents, both before and after curfew hours, endangering hapless passersby. It became customary to call ahead to an intended point of arrival to inquire if there was any word of shooting along the way, and, if so, to ascertain which route would be the best to take. Sometimes an invitation to a cocktail party or dinner would be tendered along with instructions as to which streets to avoid.

It was our particular misfortune that the *kebele* office for our district was set up in an empty shop on the ground floor of our apartment building, immediately adjacent to the entrance. Upon entering or leaving, we had to move slowly to be sure not to startle the guards, lest they fire in our direction simply as a matter of reflex.

One of the first acts of each *kebele* was to issue identity cards to people living within their district, in part to ensure that residents could not have overnight guests without the *kebele*s explicit permission. It was during this period that a proclamation was made banning the private ownership of firearms, requiring all owners to surrender them to the *kebele*, who began to enter homes in search of unlawful possession. Although such visits did not occur as often in the homes of expatriates, numerous stories circulated of a *kebele* entering homes and terrorizing occupants with threats and destruction of property.

The newest concern thus became how to dispose of ammunition and firearms without the involvement of the *kebele*. A number of friends began to take quiet drives to the countryside, where they could walk unobserved and discard their small arms and ammunition. Jack had an old rifle that he used to take on hunting expeditions. Afraid that we might need it during a crisis, he hid it carefully in a concealed storage area high above one of our bedroom closets.

The rainy season of 1975 seemed darker and more depressing than usual, thick clouds blocking the sun for days at a time. Suddenly an increasing anti-Americanism was everywhere. Posters began to appear around the city, decrying imperialism and colonialism. One day, as I headed out to the garden during a brief break in the rains, I noticed a new sign, crudely stuck to the white wall at the front of the Shelemay office building. An obscene caricature of Uncle Sam, it announced in bold, black letters, "Yankee Go Home."

I had long before given up hope of returning to the north to do research. The continued instability in the countryside made it virtually impossible to receive permission and, indeed, dangerous to travel in areas immediately outside of the capital, not to mention to Gondar, where there were frequent skirmishes. The few individuals who were allowed to travel encountered problems— friends who had established a headquarters in the north for an American welfare organization were terrorized when their small town was briefly overrun by rebel forces. They were allowed to leave, unharmed, after twenty-four hours, never to return.

Tragedies seemed to lurk everywhere. Stories circulated about young people sent to the countryside for the Zemetcha who were then stranded without food or supplies. A close colleague disappeared during a visit to Lake Tana, along with his Ethiopian assistant. They were never found, perhaps swept away by one of the sudden storms on the lake, perhaps caught in the wrong place at the wrong time. A second, supposedly accidental death of an anthropologist during a battle in the south made it clear that no one's safety could be assured.

The priests and teachers of Ambober and Tadda knew now not to expect me back, having received my letters along with gifts of heavy woolen blankets delivered by an intermediary who visited Gondar briefly just before the rains. My months in the village seemed a distant memory, even more so when, because of the unpredictable actions of the *kebele* and frequent gun battles, I became increasingly restricted to the Shelemay compound.

I had never liked driving on my own in the capital, with its crowded, bumpy roads and unpredictable pedestrian traffic. But now I felt vulnerable in a way I had not before, especially as the foreign community rapidly diminished in number and anti-

Western sentiments increased. I joked, not without a degree of bitterness, that I was living under house arrest.

We all managed as best we could with the tension, Jack and his three brothers approaching the situation with far more stoicism than I could muster. During our many hours together everyone usually made an effort to be convivial, sharing gossip or telling some of the many black jokes that circulated throughout the city. Only rarely did anyone provoke a confrontation, and then only unwittingly.

I remember once complaining angrily that I hated living with so many constraints. "Be happy that you're not in a concentration camp," snapped one of Jack's brothers. Shocked at the rebuke, I left the table in tears. I remember few other such painful exchanges. Each of us usually coped through silence and denial, too wounded to delve deeply into another's pain.

Sometimes, events themselves provided comic relief. By late August, with the properties and factories nationalized, there was little more left to take except for the increasingly stagnant export operation. We were startled, then, when one afternoon three uniformed, armed soldiers entered the Shelemay offices and asked for Jack. When he came out to meet them, one stepped forward and announced in English: "We have come to arrest your car."

"May I ask why?" Jack said, wondering if he had indeed heard correctly. He could not imagine why they would want the dark green English Rover he had acquired several years before.

"We know that you bought the car from a member of the royal family, and we would like to verify the ownership."

Unfamiliar with the automatic transmission, the soldiers asked Jack to drive the car to their headquarters, escorting him with jeeps of armed soldiers both front and rear. Eventually they arrived at the old Menelik Palace, where the PMAC had its headquarters and where surviving members of the former government and aristocracy were imprisoned.

Passing several checkpoints, each of which required a written pass, Jack was finally waved through the main gate, which quickly shut behind him. Emerging from the car, he was taken before an officer who assured him that he had nothing to worry about. The government simply wanted to clarify the legality of the sale and to ascertain whether the car had originally been imported with government funds.

"We will look into this immediately and you will have your car back soon," said the soldier. "Here is your receipt." He handed Jack a small piece of paper with illegible markings on it.

Jack never drove his car again, although he saw it once at a distance, making its way up Churchill Road, a military officer behind the wheel.

If the arrest of Jack's car was a small, somewhat ludicrous symbol of all that had been lost, other changes were not so benign. One proclamation required that, in the workplace, employers provide their employees with a place and time to hold weekly political meetings. In these gatherings, from which the employers were excluded, the workers were required to discuss the new socialist doctrine. Sometimes a representative from the Propaganda Office would attend, lecturing on current events and encouraging revolutionary zeal.

In a matter of weeks, the change of attitude became marked. Formerly close relations became strained and hostile. Jack's longtime secretary, Mulunesh, who was married to a member of the Imperial Bodyguard, the former personal army of His Imperial Majesty, had initially been frightened by the changes. As the weekly meetings continued, however, she became distant and rude. The Shelemay office, once a relaxed, even jovial environment, became quiet and tense, most matters now discussed by the brothers in private, out of earshot of the staff.

Some longtime Shelemay employees remained close, chief among them Telaye, the guard who had worked for the family for more than thirty years. Never wavering in his loyalty, he kept Salamone and Jack appraised of the many rumors echoing throughout the city.

The *kebele* had become increasingly aggressive; by September 1975, they were entering homes on the slightest excuse and intimidating people, all in the name of the revolution. On Sundays *kebele* members could often be seen standing at church gates, sent to dissuade people from going to prayers and to direct them instead to political meetings.

The *kebele* also kept a watchful eye on comings and goings, following with particular interest visits by Ethiopians to the homes of foreigners. Ethiopian friends became reluctant to visit our apartment, since they had to pass by the *kebele* guard at the door. In turn, the family became increasingly nervous about inviting over friends from the diplomatic community, easily identified by their special license plates. Most suspect of all were American diplomats, especially as the tide shifted to a new alliance with the Soviet Union. One friend from the American Embassy always made a special effort to park his car blocks away, so as not to immediately signal his identity to the guards.

When things were quiet in the city, we would sometimes accept invitations to small dinner parties at the homes of other expatriates. We were now rarely invited to the homes of Ethiopian friends, and our social network was constantly in flux, the usual multiyear tours of duty often abruptly terminated because of the deteriorating Ethiopian relationship with much of the West. Our heavily American network gave way to British friends, who were then replaced by a wave of Eastern Europeans.

What we did not lack were invitations to good-bye parties; they became the most regular social events on our calendar. People's eccentricities were magnified by the intense pressure of the revolutionary environment, providing a rather lunatic humor amid the sad farewells. At one good-bye party for an American official, his wife greeted each guest who stepped into the entry hall and asked if anyone, by any chance, had spare wooden shelves. She then pointed to the rows of empty shelf brackets, just opposite the door, that lined the hallway. Finished wood was not easily available, and in trying to pass the time during the long curfews she had used all the bookshelves in her rented house for decoupage.

Whatever the occasion, people drank. Alcohol provided one of the few escapes from the oppressive environment. With restrictions on the import of foreign wines and liquors, there was a rush on local beverages, especially a reasonably palatable wine produced by a local vineyard. Noticing that our supply was always depleted, we calculated that alcohol consumption had multiplied, with a group of seven or eight people now requiring at least that many bottles of wine. Moreover, everyone seemed to be on a different brand of tranquilizer, a source of increasing comment as the supplies at the handful of pharmacies began to diminish.

I continued to write letters home, to share whatever I could, despite the censorship, while not unduly alarming my family and friends. My parents and I developed elaborate codes, carefully worked out in letters mailed through diplomatic channels, by which I could convey information concerning our situation and our plans. Our letters were filled with news of "Dave and Nina," invented friends from "South Bend" who were notoriously poor correspondents. Jack and I ostensibly shared whatever information they sent our way in our own letters, my descriptions of their indecision and upset in fact mirroring our own.

"Dave and Nina" were unsure of when they would leave "South Bend" but were making plans and had even sent a few "gifts" along to their English relatives for Christmas. They would be sending other "mementos" to my parents in the United States, particularly recordings they had collected. We all agreed that if "Dave and Nina" were really smart, they'd just up and leave "South Bend" and stop waiting for recent "business reversals" to settle down.

The one bright spot in the last months before the rainy season was a new arrival—a now rare event—a young British woman had come to work as librarian at the British Council. I was elated to discover that Eileen Mann was an accomplished pianist. A frustrated musician who had wanted to be a composer, she was equally delighted to find a singer to accompany. We immediately began to practice, exhilarated by the possibility of making music.

I had been singing intermittently for some months with a small mixed chorus called, quite accurately, the Motley Singers. Founded and conducted by Pippa Sandford, The Brigadier's most musical daughter, we got together once a week to rehearse an odd assortment of choral pieces. When it was decided that we would put on a small choral concert at the German church, Eileen and I were invited to prepare several solos to fill out the program. Sadly, that concert was not to be. The day before the event, the pastor of the church, who had been under the mistaken impression that we were performing a concert of sacred music, was shocked to discover that I was planning to sing several Mozart arias about the hazards of love. Eileen and I were asked not to perform.

Any small flap quickly became news among the foreign community, and there was considerable indignation that we had been so abruptly removed from the program. As a result, the next month we were invited to present a concert to help raise money for the new OXFAM medical relief program in the Ogaden. Eileen and three British diplomats performed an enthusiastic rendition of the Mozart Piano Quartet in G Minor. A resident Dutch agricultural economist proved to be a creditable flutist, and he joined Eileen in playing a Vivaldi flute sonata. Eileen and I performed an assortment of German and English songs to an appreciative audience, and we were invited to perform again the following month at the British ambassador's residence. In the midst of the trauma, our music was both diversion and comfort.

An apartment became vacant in our building, and just before the nationalization of urban property, Eileen moved in. Now we could rehearse whatever the situation in the city, and we were additionally relieved of having to travel in the evening after Eileen had finished her workday. With the departure of my sisters-in-law, Eileen's presence was little short of a miracle. We played music, listened to records, and held impromptu play readings. But no sooner were we launched on our modest performing career in Addis Ababa than Eileen contracted a severe case of hepatitis and had to spend several months convalescing. Soon after, the Motley Singers disbanded as well, Pippa Sandford departing, too discouraged to remain after the loss of her beloved Mulu Farm.

One development followed another. With the PMAC now in

full control nearly a year after unseating the emperor, it was announced that a new currency would be issued. This move had long been expected, not least because the former emperor's picture was on every Ethiopian bill. People were instructed to bring in all their cash and to exchange it for new issue of the same value. The announcement caused an uproar. Many Ethiopians had large caches of money in their homes and now feared being investigated if they were to exchange large sums. As a result, many disposed of their money, throwing it away or burning it. For the only time in Ethiopia's history, fires were fed by money, not wood.

In early September the rains ended, and the *Masqal* flowers once again dotted the landscape. I longed to go north, if only for a week or two, to once again experience the Beta Israel holidays. But travel was impossible, with petrol scarce and the available supplies rationed. The Beta Israel, too, were experiencing increasing problems, their area torn by intermittent fighting and banditry. The events of the Ethiopian revolution, which ironically had restored to the Beta Israel rights lost centuries before, had proved to be the final catalyst in their desire to emigrate.

For more than a year we had kept my exit visa up to date. But in late September the wives of Greek businessmen whose supermarkets had earlier been nationalized had their exit visas revoked without warning. Our situation was quite similar and we began to worry that I, too, would not be allowed to depart. But a final event made it impossible to delay my departure any longer.

A cousin of Jack's who lived in Asmara was abducted and held for ransom. For three terrifying weeks his whereabouts were unknown and the family struggled to raise a huge sum. Finally they obtained his freedom and he was returned unharmed. Other kidnappings followed in the north, and it was rumored that they might begin in the capital as well. The number of expatriates had declined, and Americans were now regularly the objects of virulent graffiti and verbal abuse. We were afraid that the American wife of a Shelemay might provide an attractive target.

In November 1975, Jack decided that he would leave Ethiopia for good at the earliest opportunity and that there was no longer any point for both of us to remain in the quagmire. We planned to settle in the United States—I wanted to go home, and Jack had spent six happy months there a few years earlier. He wanted to live in an environment that offered the stability that had eluded him in both Aden and Ethiopia.

In the following weeks we began to empty the house of everything but those bare essentials Jack would need, selling through word of mouth our new dining room table and household items. I would take only what I could pack, giving away or selling things I had to leave behind.

Although I had already taken or sent most of my research materials out of the country, the tapes I had made in the final months remained. With no more tapes available to make extra copies, I decided that I had to hand carry the originals with me when I left. According to newly established procedures, all tapes to be taken out of the country had to be screened by the censor in a government office near the piazza. One day, with a large box of tapes, I went to the censor's office, where I was taken before an army officer. I explained that I was a student of Ethiopian music and had made these tapes with various musicians in the last few months. He looked at my residency visa, exit visa, and papers from the institute.

"What is on these tapes?" he asked, holding one up, trying to read the label.

"I'd be glad to play something for you if you wish," I replied. "They include many types of Ethiopian music, songs for the flute and the *masenqo*, styles of different provinces." I referred in passing to the Ethiopian Christian liturgical recordings that comprised the vast majority of the collection before him. "Would you like to hear *tezzeta*?" I asked casually.

"That would be nice," he answered, smiling broadly, settling back in his chair.

I rummaged through the tapes, having previously planned to play a recording of *tezzeta* I had dubbed at the beginning of one reel for just this purpose. Every Ethiopian knew *tezzeta*, a sentimental choice with its words of love. So there the censor and

I sat, listening to the song played on the tinny reel-to-reel tape recorder in his office. I thought of the many different times and places that I had heard the song—played by an *azmari* in Gondar, arranged for saxophone and keyboard at the Addis Ababa Hilton, sung by well-known singers over the radio. The song for me had come to symbolize the essence of Ethiopia and the love I felt for a country in crisis, for so many of its people, and especially for one man in particular who could no longer call it his home.

Whatever *tezzeta* meant to the censor, he appeared quite satisfied, waiting until the song ended to stop the recorder. Then he replaced the tape in its case, sealed the box, and stamped on all sides that it had been approved for export.

One remaining problem was what to do with the small group of musical instruments I had collected. I had obtained a wonderful *kebaro*, the big, booming church drum. The musicians from Orchestra Ethiopia had helped me to locate and buy several traditional instruments, including a *bagana*, the large, ten-stringed lyre, and horns from the south. Jack and I agreed that I should try to take the collection out of the country, and we found out that I had to obtain certification from the museum that the objects were not antiquities.

One day we put all the drums into the office van and drove them to the museum for examination and appraisal. All were quickly approved since none were old or valuable. But there was one problem, the official explained, as he handed over the paperwork I would need for customs.

"The drums are made of skin that still has the hair on it. You must get a veterinary certificate from the Ministry of Agriculture or you might not be able to take these into another country."

Anthrax, foot-and-mouth disease, was often found among livestock in Africa. As a result, importing countries were strict in their requirements for certification against infection, particularly for untreated hides and skins. So that is how we came to take the drums to the Ministry of Agriculture, where we carted them before several perplexed officials. For probably the first time in memory, they provided a veterinary certificate for musical instruments, stating that our drums were free of anthrax or other infection.

The day before my departure, we went to the bank to obtain the limit of $600 in traveler's checks that were allowed a departing permanent resident. We also needed approval in my passport for the tape recorder and the shortwave radio I wished to take. My request was closely scrutinized by a bank official, who kept insisting that I could not take out items bought with foreign currency.

"I bought these items myself outside the country before I was a resident," I insisted, upset by the man's refusal to approve my simple request. "It is important that I take them with me."

"Would you say that you are emotionally attached to the radio?" he said sharply, noting my increasing agitation.

"Yes, I am emotionally attached to the radio," I replied with difficulty, humiliated at the entire process, remembering the ease with which I had entered the country so long before.

That night I packed my bags, placing Yosef Berhanu's handwritten Amharic-Hebrew dictionary at the very bottom of a large, deep bag. He had begged me to take it to Israel for him and to give it to his son for safekeeping. Concerned that the book, if shown to the censor, would arouse too much suspicion, I decided to risk taking it anyway, hidden at the bottom of a bag that I felt certain no one would examine.

Late that last night, Jack and I opened a bottle of champagne, drinking to our hopes for the future. Early the next morning, Jack drove me along Bole Road to the airport. Embracing him one last time, I checked in, my shaky composure disintegrating when the guard carrying out a body search tried to steal my watch. Crying, I rushed out of the curtained booth, my tears distracting the officials and perhaps ensuring that my suitcases and box of tapes would pass through customs with only the most cursory inspection.

I walked through passport control and climbed up the broad, black-tiled stairs that led to the departure lounge, filled with its duty-free Ethiopian mementos. As I reached the top and opened the door, I turned and looked down. Through the large window at the bottom of the steps I could see Jack standing in his light-blue suit, one hand pressed against the glass in a gesture of farewell. I breathed deeply, turned away, and passed through the door, closing it behind me.

POSTSCRIPT

After nearly three years of involuntary separation, Jack was finally permitted to leave Ethiopia in 1978 and join me in New York. Today we live in Connecticut, where I am a professor of music at Wesleyan University. Jack is engaged in the leather business in New York City.

General Habte was released from an Ethiopian prison in 1989.

Marigeta Yohannes continues in his role as a master singer of the Ethiopian church.

Father Marqos left Ethiopia in 1977 and has since lived in exile in the United States.

Tesemma left Ethiopia and now lives in exile in Europe.

Priest Mika'el and Wezero Alganesh now live in Israel, as did Alaqa Gete and Yosef Berhanu until their deaths in the late 1980s. In May 1991 the revolutionary Ethiopian government was overthrown and a massive airlift took most of the remaining Beta Israel community from Ethiopia to Israel.

Most of the Adenite Jewish community has left Ethiopia for London, Israel, Italy, or the United States. Of the Shelemay family, Aviva, Ruth, and Yona remained in Israel, Alicia is in Toronto, and Danny has settled in Connecticut. Moshe died during 1984 in Israel, as did Ben, in 1985. Only Salamone remains in Ethiopia.

SELECTED BIBLIOGRAPHY

Abbink, G. J. 1984. *The Falashas in Ethiopia and Israel: The Problem of Ethnic Assimilation.* Nijmegen, Netherlands: Institute for Cultural and Social Anthropology.

Abu-Lughod, Lila. 1986. *Veiled Sentiments. Honor and Poetry in a Bedouin Society.* Berkeley and Los Angeles: University of California Press.

Aešcoly, A. Z. 1973. *Sefer Hafalašim.* 2d ed. Jerusalem: Reuben Mass Press.

Berger, Natalia, and Kay Kaufman Shelemay. 1986. *The Jews of Ethiopia. A People in Transition.* Tel Aviv and New York: Beth Hatefutsoth and the Jewish Museum.

Bowen, Elenore Smith. [1954]1964. *Return to Laughter: An Anthropological Novel.* New York: Doubleday.

Briggs, Jean. 1970. *Never in Anger.* Cambridge: Harvard University Press.

Cesara, Manda. 1982. *Reflections of a Woman Anthropologist: No Hiding Place.* New York: Academic Press.

Clifford, James, and George E. Marcus. 1986. *Writing Culture: The Poetics and Politics of Ethnography.* Berkeley and Los Angeles: University of California Press.

Crapanzano, Vincent. 1980. *Tuhami: Portrait of a Moroccan.* Chicago: University of Chicago Press.

Doubleday, Veronica. 1990. *Three Women of Herat.* Austin: University of Texas Press.

Fabian, Johannes. 1983. *Time and the Other: How Anthropology Makes Its Object.* New York: Columbia University Press.

Faitlovitch, Jacques. 1910. *Quer durch Abessinien: Meine zweiter Reise zu den Falaschas.* Berlin: Verlag von M. Poppelauer.

Flad, Johann M. 1869. *The Falashas (Jews) of Abyssinia.* Trans. S. P. Goodhart. London: William Macintosh.

Gamst, Frederick G. 1969. *The Qemant: A Pagan-Hebraic Peasantry of Ethiopia.* New York: Holt, Rinehart & Winston.

Golde, Peggy. [1970]1986. "Introduction." In *Women in the Field.* 2d ed. Ed. Peggy Golde. Berkeley and Los Angeles: University of California Press, 1–15.

Halévy, Joseph. 1877. "Travels in Abyssinia." Trans. James Picciotto. In *Miscellany of Hebrew Literature*. Ed. A. Lowy. Publication of the Society of Hebrew Literature, 2d ser. London: Wertheimer, Lea & Co.

Harbeson, John W. 1988. *The Ethiopian Transformation: The Quest for the Post-Imperial State*. Boulder, Colo.: Westview Press.

Heilbrun, Carolyn G. 1979. *Reinventing Womanhood*. New York: W.W. Norton & Co.

————. 1988. *Writing a Woman's Life*. New York: W.W. Norton & Co.

Hess, Robert L. 1969. "Towards a History of the Falasha." In *Eastern African History*. Ed. Daniel F. McCall, Norman R. Bennett, and Jeffrey Butler. Boston University Papers on Africa, vol. 3. New York: Frederick A. Praeger, 107–32.

Kaplan, Steven. 1984. *The Monastic Holy Man and the Christianization of Ethiopia*. Wiesbaden: Franz Steiner Verlag.

————, and Shoshana Ben-Dor. 1988. *Ethiopian Jewry: An Annotated Bibliography*. Jerusalem: Ben-Zvi Institute.

Kessler, David. 1982. *The Falashas: The Forgotten Jews of Ethiopia*. New York: Africana Publishing Co.

Leslau, Wolf. 1951. *Falasha Anthology*. Yale Judaica Series, vol. 6. New Haven: Yale University Press.

Levine, Donald N. 1965. *Wax and Gold: Tradition and Innovation in Ethiopian Society*. Chicago: University of Chicago Press.

————. 1974. *Greater Ethiopia*. Chicago: University of Chicago Press.

Marcus, George, and Michael Fischer. 1986. *Anthropology as Cultural Critique*. Chicago: University of Chicago Press.

Messing, Simon D. 1982. *The Story of the Falashas*. Hamden, Conn.: Balshon Printing Co.

Pankhurst, Richard. 1968. *Economic History of Ethiopia*. Addis Ababa: Haile Sellassie I University Press.

Pankhurst, Sylvia. 1955. *Ethiopia: A Cultural History*. Essex: Lalibela House.

Park, Robert E. 1928. "Human Migration and the Marginal Man." *American Journal of Sociology* 33 (6): 881–93.

Payne, Eric. 1972. *Ethiopian Jews: The Story of a Mission*. London: Vincent House.

Provisional Administrative Military Council. 1975. *The Ethiopian Revolution*. Addis Ababa.

Rabinow, Paul. 1977. *Reflections on Fieldwork in Morocco*. Berkeley and Los Angeles: University of California Press.

Rapoport, Louis. 1980. *The Lost Jews: Last of the Ethiopian Falashas*. New York: Stein and Day.

Sergew Hable Sellassie. 1972. *Ancient and Medieval Ethiopian History to 1270*. Addis Ababa: United Printers.

Shack, William A. 1979. "Open Systems and Closed Boundaries: The Ritual Process of Stranger Relations in New African States." In *Strangers in African Societies*. Ed. William A. Shack and Elliot P. Skinner. Berkeley and Los Angeles: University of California Press, 37–47.

———, and Elliot P. Skinner, eds. 1979. *Strangers in African Societies*. Berkeley and Los Angeles: University of California Press.

Shelemay, Kay Kaufman. 1978a. "A Quarter Century in the Life of a Falasha Prayer." *Yearbook of the International Folk Music Council* 10: 83–108.

———. 1978b. "Rethinking Falasha Liturgical History." *Proceedings of the Fifth International Conference of Ethiopian Studies (B)*. Ed. Robert Hess. Chicago, 397–410.

———. 1980a. "Continuity and Change in the Liturgy of the Falashas." *Modern Ethiopia: Proceedings of the Fifth International Conference of Ethiopian Studies (A)*. Ed. Joseph Tubiana. Rotterdam: A. A. Balkema, 479–89.

———. 1980b. " 'Historical Ethnomusicology': Reconstructing Falasha Liturgical History." *Ethnomusicology* 24 (May): 233–58.

———. 1980–81. "*Seged*: A Falasha Pilgrimage Festival." *Musica Judaica* 3:42–62.

———. 1982a. "*Zēmā*: A Concept of Sacred Music in Ethiopia." *The World of Music* 3:52–67.

———. 1982b. "The *Lālibēloč*: Musical Mendicants in Ethiopia." *Journal of African Studies* 9 (Fall): 128–38.

———. 1982–83. "Music and Text of the Falasha Sabbath." *Orbis Musicae* 8:3–22.

———. 1983. "A New System of Musical Notation in Ethiopia." In *Ethiopian Studies Dedicated to Wolf Leslau*. Ed. Stanislav Segert and Andras J. E. Bodrogligeti. Wiesbaden: Otto Harrassowitz, 571–82.

———. 1985. "Folk Memory and Jewish Identity: The Falasha Dilemma." In *Solomon Goldman Lectures: Perspectives in Jewish Learning*. Ed. Nathaniel Stampher. Chicago: Spertus College Press, 43–54.

———. 1986. "A Comparative Study: Jewish Liturgical Forms in the Falasha Liturgy?" *Yuval* 5 (Jerusalem: Magnes Press): 372–404.

———. [1986]1989. *Music, Ritual, and Falasha History*. East Lansing: Michigan State University Press.

———, and Peter Jeffery. In press. *Ethiopian Christian Chant: An Anthology*. Madison, Wis.: A-R Editions, Inc.

Shostak, Marjorie. 1981. *Nisa: The Life and Words of a !Kung Woman*. Cambridge: Harvard University Press.

Showalter, Elaine. 1982. "Feminist Criticism in the Wilderness." In *Writing and Sexual Difference*. Ed. Elizabeth Abel. Chicago: University of Chicago Press, 9–35.

Simmel, Georg. [1908]1950. "The Stranger." In *The Sociology of Georg Simmel*. Trans. and ed. Kurt H. Wolff. New York: Free Press, 402–8.

Simoons, Frederick J. 1960. *Northwest Ethiopia: Peoples and Economy*. Madison: University of Wisconsin Press.

Taddesse Tamrat. 1972. *Church and State in Ethiopia, 1270–1527*. Oxford: Clarendon Press.

Turner, Edith. 1987. *The Spirit and the Drum: A Memoir of Africa*. Tucson: University of Arizona Press.

Ullendorff, Edward. 1956. "Hebraic-Jewish Elements in Abyssinian (Monophysite) Christianity." *Journal of Semitic Studies* 1:216–56.

———. 1968. *Ethiopia and the Bible: The Schweich Lectures,1967*. London: Oxford University Press, for the British Academy.

———. 1973. *The Ethiopians: An Introduction to Country and People*. 3d ed. London: Oxford University Press.

Useem, John, Ruth Useem, and John Donoghue. 1963. "Men in the Middle of the Third Culture: The Roles of American and Non-Western People in Cross-cultural Administration." *Human Organization* 22(3): 169–79.

Wax, Rosalie. 1971. *Doing Fieldwork: Warnings and Advice*. Chicago: University of Chicago Press.

Weidman, Hazel Hitson. [1970]1986. "On Ambivalence and the Field." In *Women in the Field*. 2d ed. Ed. Peggy Golde. Berkeley and Los Angeles: University of California Press, 237–63.

INDEX

A Note on the Author

KAY KAUFMAN SHELEMAY received a Ph.D. in musicology from the University of Michigan and is now on the Department of Music faculty at Wesleyan University. She is the author of *Music, Ritual, and Falasha History*, winner of the ASCAP–Deems Taylor Award and the Prize of the International Musicological Society.